The literature of exhaustion

This book is dedicated to my parents, Mr. and Mrs. John Stark.

The literature of exhaustion

Borges, Nabokov, and Barth

by John O. Stark

Duke University Press
Durham, N.C.   1974

© 1974, Duke University Press

L.C.C. card no. 73–92536

I.S.B.N. 0–8223–0316–7

Printed in the United States
by Heritage Printers, Inc.

Acknowledgements

For help with this book I am indebted to Wayne Kvam, Louis Paskoff, Lewis Fried, Mrs. Carol Thompson of Duke University Press, and my wife Faye.

ERRATA

Page 90, line 33: *For* Appel *read* Jeffrey Leonard
Page 92, line 5: *For* Appel *read* Leonard
Page 104, line 26: *For* Appel *read* George Steiner

Contents

Introduction

The combination of Jorge Luis Borges, Vladimir Nabokov, and John Barth seems bizarre if one considers their nationalities or lives. The first two were born in the same year, 1899, but one is an Argentinian who spent some of his formative years in Spain, and the other is a Russian who has lived in America, England, and Germany, finally settling in Switzerland. Even if these two writers share a few personal characteristics, Barth—thirty-one years younger and distinctly American—does not seem to belong with them. One who turns to their fiction, however, will see many resemblances among them.

In his seminal essay "The Literature of Exhaustion" Barth himself supplies the best label for this group.[1] The identifying characteristic of the Literature of Exhaustion, he states, is that writers of it pretend that it is next to impossible to write original—perhaps any—literature. In other words, some writers use as a theme for new works of literature the agonizing hypothesis that literature is finished. "Exhaustion," then, has two meanings in Barth's essay: one, that literature is, or is nearly, used up; the other, that, given its current condition, writers should invent and exhaust possibilities and thus create for literature an infinite scope. They can accomplish this latter purpose by writing about the present exhausted state of literature, thereby making their original hypothesis a paradox. The greatest writers can do this and at the same time write validly about nonaesthetic matters. Barth deals with Borges at length and mentions Nabokov, thus suggesting that he and they can validly be considered together. He also begins to spell out specific features of the Literature of Exhaustion, such as the topic of dreams and the image of the labyrinth.

Two questions immediately arise about this label: how much of the work of each writer does it explain? and how does the work it encompasses relate to other kinds of literature? The Literature of Exhaustion almost totally accounts for Borges's work. Although to a certain extent *Dr. Brodie's Report* and scattered pieces throughout his career do not belong to this kind of literature, nearly all his writing does. Moreover, the rubrics of the Literature of Exhaustion will explain all but a few aspects of most of Borges's individual works. The ease with which he can be labeled suggests limitations in his work that make him less than a truly major writer, despite the fascinating qualities of his work. Barth, too, fits this label fairly completely. His work develops in an orderly fashion from book to book, his first two novels setting the stage for his Literature of Exhaustion phase rather than fully participating in it. Although the later books exude an enormous gusto that intrigues readers and defies classification, one can best understand the central concerns of Barth's work by considering him in this category. Nabokov also went through an orderly development in his career. Some aspects of the Literature of Exhaustion appear in his early novels, but he wrote an enormous number of books before the three that belong to this tradition. Many of his distinguishing characteristics, like his wistful portraits of aliens and his remarkable prose style, fall outside my concerns here. This largeness indicates that he, a truly major writer, has done more important work than have the other two. In other words, this study deals with Borges, Barth, and a part of Nabokov.

As to this label's relation to other labels, several critics have seen in contemporary fiction tendencies similar to the ones that I will analyze. Occasionally some of these critics mention one or more of the three writers in this study. Demonstrating the relation between my label and others will show why these writers form a school distinct enough to be analyzed and also will occasionally suggest other perspectives from which they can be viewed. Robert Jay

Lifton, in a suggestive essay, "Protean Man," deals briefly but provocatively with several novelists.[2] In updating David Reisman's picture of the other-directed man, he claims that several social and cultural changes, such as the flood of information from the media and a loosening of the ties with cultural tradition, have caused a great number of people to become protean, to continually change their personality types. In addition to the obvious consequences for characterization in novels, Lifton points out a tendency to emphasize process, rather than static meanings, in art. He describes a "literature of mockery" that attacks a wide variety of targets. This trend, exemplified by Camp and Black Humor, which have died out, prepares for the more specific and careful diagnosis that the protean writers make. In addition to favoring process over completion and denying that the world and the persons in it have stability, as do the protean writers, Borges, Nabokov, and Barth go further to argue that the world has very little, if any, reality. These latter writers, rather than locating the trouble in psychological trends, examine the nature of literature. In other words, Lifton describes an earlier trend than the Literature of Exhaustion, though one that likely was a forerunner of it.

At least three critics have mentioned contemporary literature's yearning for "silence." One of them, Susan Sontag, promulgates a theory of contemporary literature that closely resembles Barth's view in "The Literature of Exhaustion," so her analysis clearly relates to mine.[3] She, too, writes about art assuming its primacy over the everyday world: "from the promotion of the arts into 'art' comes the leading myth about art, that of the absoluteness of the artist's activity" (p. 4). Following this stage, art turns into anti-art or silence, which "proposes a mood of ultimacy" (p. 6). Her "ultimacy" recalls Barth's "exhaustion," and she offers the same solution that Barth does: "discovering that one has nothing to say, one seeks a way to say *that*" (p. 12). Without mentioning Borges, Nabokov, or Barth specifically, she identifies some of the characteristics of their work: war with the audience (compare the false clues that Nabokov sprinkles throughout *Lolita*), self-consciousness, the dream of an ahistorical literature, and disinterest in communicating meanings.

In *Styles of Radical Will*, and even more in *Against Interpretation*, she argues that the existence of this kind of literature should encourage critics to avoid analyzing the meanings of literature. Her position, however, takes perfectly seriously a hypothesis that the writers of the Literature of Exhaustion merely use pragmatically as a basis for producing more work. Rather than abdicating their function of explicating meaning, critics of this kind of literature should pay more careful attention to its aesthetic themes and to the ways technical devices are used to reinforce these themes.

As his title suggests, in *Language and Silence* George Steiner describes several of the same qualities that Susan Sontag has noticed.[4] He spends more time than she does sketching in the social changes that have contributed to, if not caused, modern writers' craving for silence. According to Steiner, the problems of current artists, particularly novelists, are "grounded in historical circumstances, in a late stage of linguistic and formal civilization in which the expressive achievements of the past seem to weigh exhaustively on the possibilities of the present, in which word and genre seem tarnished" (p. 49). The weight of past literature, as reflected by the hypothesis that original literature cannot be written, becomes the basis for the Literature of Exhaustion. In addition to seeking silence, writers, according to Steiner, can also cope with this situation by trying to turn literature into either light or music. In "Silence and the Poet" he analyzes interesting passages that show these three desires.

Steiner raises an interesting question: to what extent have changes in social and cultural conditions produced the changes in literature that many critics have seen? Barth correctly states that the writers of the Literature of Exhaustion focus not on social problems but on literary problems. This very choice of emphasis, as well as some of the themes and techniques that follow from it, however, possibly have social causes. One could begin by identifying these causes, but to do so would distort this literature by subjecting it to precisely the kind of scrutiny that it so carefully tries to avoid. I will examine it on its own terms; once this is done others may wish to assign social and cultural causes to it.

The other alternative that Steiner mentions, journalistic fiction, accounts for a good deal more of contemporary writing. Like Lifton, he attributes much importance to the media's ability to saturate its audience: "the novel now has to compete with media of dramatic presentation far more 'authentic', far easier to assimilate" (p. 81). On the other hand, "The great mass of current fiction is reportage —less convincing, less acute, less impressive on the memory, than are current works of history, of biography, of social and political narrative" (p. 81). Thus Capote's *In Cold Blood*, the recent books of Norman Mailer, and many other contemporary works of prose literature respond in their own way to the crisis in fiction that also leads to the Literature of Exhaustion. These writers, however, search for new realistic subject matter on which they can use their old techniques. Their subject matter thus differs significantly from that of the Literature of Exhaustion, and they do much less experimenting with techniques.

The third chronicler of this trend toward silence, Ihab Hassan, sounds this theme in two books: *The Literature of Silence* and *The Dismemberment of Orpheus*.[5] In the prologue to the first of these books he describes the present state of fiction in much the same way as Barth and the previously mentioned critics. Before arriving at the alternative that most interests him, Hassan discusses the possibilities of conceiving literature as a game (which fits many of the techniques of Borges, Nabokov, and Barth), as action (an alternative that Richard Poirier describes at length), and as journalism. Hassan defines silence as "the disruption of all connection between language and reality" (p. 22). This absolute distinction between these two domains precedes the Literature of Exhaustion's ultimate argument that the domain of language and literature paradoxically contains all reality and that the "real" world contains none. He claims that writers seek silence by trying to do without the traditional elements of fiction, such as character, plot, metaphor, and meaning. This idea helps place several contemporary French novelists—Sarraute, Butor, Robbe-Grillet, and others—in relation to the Literature of Exhaustion. For example, their creation of two-dimensional characters may be influenced by Husserl's notion that the self ultimately cannot be known. In contrast, the Literature of Exhaustion argues that the self, like the rest of everyday reality, is not truly real. These French writers and the other practitioners of the Literature of Silence differ somewhat from Borges, Nabokov, and Barth also in that the latter three try not to do without these elements but to point out their artifice, thereby hoping to prove that the imaginative world, not the everyday world, is real. Hassan's work on Beckett suggests that this writer would be the logical choice if a fourth writer were to be added to my study.

In *The Dismemberment of Orpheus* Hassan argues that contemporary novelists, due to stresses in our culture, conceive fiction to be either all or nothing. The Literature of Exhaustion falls in the first category, the Literature of Silence in the second. Hassan claims, however, that very similar writing results from both premises, so they ultimately become nearly indistinguishable rather than opposite. For example, writers of both types subvert traditional literary forms and try to "de-realize" the world (p. 13). This latter goal is the dominant one for writers of the Literature of Exhaustion. In "Fiction and Future: An Extravaganza for Voice and Tape," a more recent work, Hassan proposes a slightly different dichotomy to explain current fictional trends: the Literature of Exhaustion and the Fantastic Novel.[6] The Literature of Exhaustion attempts to subvert itself, he contends, whereas the Fantastic Novel attempts to transcend itself. It may be better to say that the Literature of Exhaustion begins by pretending that literature already has been subverted. He usefully shows how several young, less well known writers relate to these two opposite kinds of literature, which he assumes will eventually merge. Anyone who wishes to apply the ideas in this book to younger writers should read Hassan's essay.

Richard Poirier discusses "performing," which resembles Hassan's idea of the novel as action.[7] He defines it as a self-discovering activity, "energy which cannot arrange itself within the existing order of things" (p. xv). To be specific, he urges critics to try to discern a writer's activity while producing a work, what it felt like to write it, rather than what significance the work has. Poirier makes some very perceptive readings based on this admonition and offers interesting and useful pedagogical advice. A reader of the Literature of Exhaustion should follow Poirier's advice and attend to the writer and not to his imitation of the quotidian world, but he need not watch the writer's performance as carefully as the imaginative world the writer builds and the ways he attacks the real world. When Poirier draws corollaries from his main thesis, however, the Literature of Performance and the Literature of Exhaustion begin to converge. For example, he talks about a writer building a realm of his own rather than imitating a given realm. Even more striking, he says that "the human imagination . . . is impossibly entangled in its own creations" (p. 21). Thus, like Barth, he believes that a condition of ultimacy faces the contemporary novelist. He also makes points relevant to the Literature of Exhaustion when he describes contemporary writers trying to defeat time. Poirier mentions the prevalence of parody in contemporary fiction, a condition that applies to the Literature of Exhaustion's spoofing of established genres in order to demonstrate the existence of ultimacy. In short, like Sontag, he sees trends in contemporary literature that are similar to those in the Literature of Exhaustion, but his advice to critics applies better to those who wish to examine slightly different literature.

Robert Scholes presents in *The Fabulators* another view of the contemporary literary scene.[8] By fabulative literature he means literature that insists on its unreality, that announces its artifice. Clearly, the Literature of Exhaustion flaunts its distinctness from the "real" world, claiming to be real in a truer sense. Scholes mentions that the fabulators oppose realism, which makes them akin to the writers of the Literature of Exhaustion. When he identifies the motive for fabulation, the unbearable weight of the knowledge of tradition that stifles writers today, he agrees with Barth. He correctly claims that myth and allegory exist in the one book that he and I both discuss, *Giles Goat-Boy*, but they appear only rarely in the other works of the Literature of Exhaustion. Scholes's emphasis on the comic qualities of the literature he discusses contrasts effectively with some overly solemn critical analyses of very witty writers: those he analyzes as well as Borges, Nabokov, and Barth. Not simply because he discusses *Giles Goat-Boy*, his analysis resembles mine more closely than do those of the other critics.

Scholes attributes the comedy he mentions mainly to a realization by these writers of fabulation's limits. In other words, much of the comedy results from self-parody. If so, is the Literature of Exhaustion also merely a spinning of wheels until fiction can begin moving forward again? and do these writers secretly know this? Borges's and Barth's demonstrations that the world is unreal do have an element of obsessiveness about them, even occasionally an air of futility. A reader sometimes believes that the two are preparing the way and that other writers will have to make the breakthrough. Nabokov, on the contrary, seems to control the Literature of Exhaustion rather than to be controlled by it, to be able to use it when it suits his purposes. Even Borges and Barth, however, direct almost all of their satire outward rather than against themselves. The comedy of these three writers differs from the kind Scholes describes.

Two critics discuss the fear that modern writers have of closed systems. Elizabeth Sewell has seen that writers like Edward Lear and Lewis Carroll avoid them by writing nonsense, "a collection of words or events which in their arrangements do not fit into some recognized system in a particular mind."[9] Tony Tanner has recognized a similar attitude in more recent works, citing many negative comments by contemporary American writers on entropy.[10] Borges, Nabokov, and Barth particularly dislike symmetrical closed systems, as well as modes of literature, such as realism, that cannot produce infinite possibilities. Their strategies for avoiding closure, however, differ from those of the writers that Sewell and Tanner mention.

Now that I have, at least hazily, drawn its borders, I can begin to discuss the Literature of Exhaustion by itself. In order to clarify the similarities among the three writers, I will organize each of the sections in the same way, beginning each time by clarifying a few ideas and methods that relate closely to the basic assumptions of the Literature of Exhaustion. A reader can most quickly understand these writers by noticing the Chinese boxes, and, less important, the infinite regresses, they construct. Our authors use these clever tactics at first to make "reality" problematical and then to suggest that the "real" world has no reality. They also attack literary realism and argue that literature should primarily be about literature, not about everyday reality.

Once this philosophical and technical framework has been explained, one's attention logically should turn to the themes of this kind of literature. Time, the most important theme, presents problems to these writers. They must attack this basic constituent of the realistic conception of the world, but although they desire to create nontemporal art, they cannot escape the inevitably temporal nature of literature. This contradiction weakens their attacks. Borges and Barth also treat negatively the companion theme of time, memory, because they recognize the relations between these two themes and between memory and *past* reality. To clarify this last recognition, one who admits the possibility of memory also admits that the real world once did exist; otherwise it could not be remembered. Though these three writers do not acknowledge it, the oppression of the past because of the superabundance of information now available may also influence their actions. For the same reason, but much less frequently, these writers attack the common notions about space. Because the Literature of Exhaustion begins with the hypothesis that literature has used up all its possibilities, themes of limitation and lack of limitation abound in it. For example, these writers negatively treat symmetry, a theme of limitation. Conversely, they positively treat the theme of infinity. In other words, these three writers, like many others, prefer open systems to closed systems. All these themes form part of one, overarching theme: the relation between literature and reality. Occasionally they develop directly this general theme, which is perhaps the dominant one in contemporary fiction.

They also convey their themes partly by means of a few images: the labyrinth, the mirror, and the circle. They usually treat the second of these images negatively, because it repeats and therefore limits. The labyrinth, which pervades this literature, and the circle are ambiguous and more complex. The meanings of these images relate very closely to the themes already identified. Character, plot, and style, besides their intrinsic interest, become pawns in the battle against reality and realism. These writers use their characters, who in many instances are two-dimensional, to attack the notion of individual identity. Similarly, the style of these three writers calls attention to itself, which in turn makes it undeniable that literature creates artifice rather than imitating reality.

Finally, Nabokov and, to a lesser extent, Barth allow a traditional theme, a staple of the realistic novel, to appear in their work. They offer love as a solution but not until after they make their case against realism and commonsense notions of reality. As Poirier says, after a writer fights his arduous battle with the condition of ultimacy he earns the right to assert simple virtues (p. 22). These writers, however, have much more interest in the arduous battle.

Jorge Luis Borges

Borges, the archetypal writer of the Literature of Exhaustion, should be considered first. From his earliest prose almost to the present he has most consistently written in this vein. His latest book, *Dr. Brodie's Report*, contains realistic short stories, although he uses in them some of his characteristic themes and techniques.[1] Both Nabokov and Barth at first wrote fairly conventional and realistic novels, but even their early work contains features of the Literature of Exhaustion. Moreover, both Barth and Nabokov in their most recent works are concerned in part with matters very different from the Literature of Exhaustion, and this concern possibly forebodes a transition by them to a new kind of literature.

This is no place for a systematic biography of Borges, or of the other two writers. In the first place, ample biographical material on Borges and Nabokov already exists, some of it written by others, the most important and interesting written, naturally enough, by these writers themselves. The latter kind includes Borges's autobiographical sketch in *The New Yorker* and Nabokov's *Speak, Memory* and its earlier versions.[2] Barth's life can be pieced together fairly satisfactorily from a few incomplete sources. More importantly, these writers oppose in theory autobiographical and other kinds of realistic fiction. Occasionally, however, they ignore their theory, and it will be interesting to allude in passing to biographical data in order to show the tension between their lives and art.

Besides this occasional discrepancy between theory and practice, their nonfiction contains a few inconsistencies. Happily, these contradictions do not at all harm their work, because they do not try to instruct. Rather they use the basic ideas of the Literature of Exhaustion as subject matter, not dogma. They choose ideas for their literary value, not for their cogency. For example, Borges's use of this criterion explains his exotic taste in literature: he once placed heavy emphasis, in a British Literature course he taught, on William Morris. Also, it should be apparent that a writer can use only as an interesting and useful hypothesis, not as doctrine, the first proposition of the Literature of Exhaustion: that authors can no longer write original literature and perhaps cannot write any literature.

This hypothesis about literature, which Barth identifies in his essay, provides the key to Borges's writing. Unfortunately, the failure of nearly all critics to use it has caused inadequate analyses of his work. Two critics have made limited use of this key. L. S. Dembo got Borges himself to identify the key to his work, albeit cryptically, when Borges said of *Ficciones:* "I wonder if there is a single original line in the book. I suppose a source can be found for every line I've written, or perhaps that's what we call inventing—mixing up memories. I don't think we're capable of creation in the way that God created the world."[3] Unfortunately this interview ends here. Similarly, Borges has recently cited William Morris's belief that "the essential stories of man's imagination had long since been told and that by now the storyteller's craft lay in rethinking and retelling them."[4] John Updike, who has also written one of the most perceptive articles on Nabokov, has used this key most expertly, although still only briefly. Early in his article on Borges, Updike announces that "Borges' narrative innovations spring from a clear sense of technical crisis. . . . he seems to be the man for whom literature has no future."[5] However, most of the time Updike develops, skillfully, other lines of analysis.

A critic can most quickly clarify Borges's work, and simultaneously explain the basic features of the Literature of Exhaustion, by describing the Chinese box arrangements in some of his works. Ana Maria Barrenechea has seen them in "Tlön, Uqbar, Orbis Tertius": "The story is constructed like a Chinese Box: unreal worlds included one within the other and then, in turn, within the earth, which disintegrates on contact with such phantasmagorias."[6] However, she errs in the second half of her statement, because the earth does not disintegrate in the story, and she does not develop her insight in regard to either this story or others. Rather, she catalogues elements in Borges's work. She has, however, hit upon the most important feature of his work and the most typical and revealing of his fictions. Ronald Christ, too, briefly mentions the Chinese boxes in Borges's work.[7]

Each box in one of his systems represents either a real or imaginary state of being. The plot of the fiction makes clear the place of each box by showing which boxes it encloses and which boxes enclose it. In "Tlön, Uqbar, Orbis Tertius" the largest, outermost box is Borges, the maker of the whole arrangement. The story itself is the next box, as one looks inside, and in it lies the border between reality and imagination, as one commonly understands these terms. This box is real because it exists in print, imaginary because Borges created it. Next comes the box of the secret society, although the reported inclusion of real people like Berkeley in the society gives it an aura of reality. The society creates the next two boxes: Uqbar, an imaginary land, and Tlön, another imaginary land that supposedly exists in Uqbar's literature. To understand the crucial Tlön layer one must make this visual representation more elaborate by imagining paths leading from this box. One path leads further inward to another box, Orbis Tertius, one more imaginary world. Another leads to the philosophical systems of Tlön. Another leads to the hrönir, an annex of the Tlön box built on the side toward the realistic section of the system. Because human minds create them the hrönir are imaginary, but because of their substantiality they are real. The fourth path from the Tlön box, representing the cone and compass, leads all the way back to the real world, where these objects intrude.

The differences among these four alternatives show what literary exhaustion means. The cone and compass are immediately exhausted—in other words, they cannot be used anymore for literary purposes—because they are material objects and appear in the real world, which cannot be extended in any significant sense. The hrönir and the philosophical systems, being imaginary, can each generate one more layer, but then they are exhausted and do not make possible another box. These three paths represent "exhaustion" in one sense of the word: a condition in which all possibilities have been used up. Orbis Tertius represents exhaustion in the other sense: the method that was used to create it can be used to create an infinite number of possibilities. That is, one can imagine worlds inside it ad infinitum.

Thus, Borges has written a story that belongs to the Literature of Exhaustion because he has based it on a belief that literary possibilities—symbolized by objects in the story—are used up, and he has employed this hypothesis to produce another work of fiction and to imply that the imagination can create endless and inexhaustible possibilities. This story makes another point about the imagination in addition to proclaiming its infinity, and also resolves the apparent contradiction at the base of this kind of literature, by implying that the realms of reality and imagination are less distinct than most people believe. That is, finally the imagination is inexhaustible because it spills over into "reality." The Chinese box system of this story reveals this attribute of imagination: one layer is both real and imaginary; other layers belong to one of these categories but also seem to belong to the other. By looking as naively as possible at this sophisticated arrangement one can pop it into focus, just as a quick second viewing often makes clear the meaning of a visual puzzle. This second glance should reveal that everything in the story as story (rather than as print on a page) is imaginary because Borges created it. Because a reader almost certainly will forget this obvious fact as he tries to sort out the real and imaginary elements in the story and then will realize it again suddenly, Borges dramatically makes his point that these realms cannot be separated at all. He sets this almost inescapable trap for the reader because, as a writer, he believes that the imagination is superior to reality.

Borges uses other Chinese box systems to prove the same points. In "Theme of the Traitor and the Hero" the outermost two boxes again are the same: Borges and the story. Then comes a narrator, Ryan, who seems indistinguishable from the narrative voice that one hears at the beginning of the story. The fourth box contains the main narrative of the story, and the fifth, because aspects of the fourth repeat it, is *Macbeth* and *Julius Caesar*. Strangely, the second and fifth boxes have exactly the same mixture of reality and imagination so that a reader has even more trouble here distinguishing between these two domains than he has in "Tlön, Uqbar, Orbis Tertius." A further problem arises when one tries to place Shakespeare in the scheme. Most readers would be tempted to say that his box lies inside the box that contains *Macbeth* and *Julius Caesar*, but then how can a nonautobiographical work enclose its author? Placing the Shakespeare box there will also make a symmetrical arrangement of two mirrors endlessly reflecting each other with Borges and Shakespeare on the ends, their works inside them, and Ryan in the middle. Borges would not accept this last property, because it duplicates rather than creates. In any case, a reader with conventional beliefs about reality and imagination will find them severely shaken if he reads this story attentively.

In "The Zahir" Borges makes a Chinese box arrangement by using the familiar device of the story within a story, but these stories relate to each other and to some themes in a typically Borgesian way. The frame story's narrator is writing a fantasy that strikingly revivifies the tradition of metaphors that begins with the Anglo-Saxon kennings. These powerful tropes have recently fascinated Borges so much that he has begun to study the language in which they are constructed. Within the frame story, which is brightly ornamented with these metaphors, lies an account of the narrator's discovery of a Zahir, an object that recapitulates, and eventually can replace, the whole universe. Almost at the end of the story appears a reference to the Sufis doggedly reciting names till they become meaningless. These three main elements in the story—the kennings, the Zahir, and the Sufis' repetition of words—all show that language and therefore literature can replace life. The kennings, "enigmatic circumlocutions," make the world seem somewhat eerie and unreal (*Labyrinths*, p. 160). Borges provides two examples: "sword-water" for blood and "serpent-bed" for gold, the latter being even more fanciful than most Anglo-Saxon kennings. The Sufis' repetition makes things in the world seem meaningless by making them seem to be purely linguistic phenomena. The Zahir at first does not appear to be related to literature or language, but the most important reference to it does make this connection: "I shall no longer perceive the universe: I shall perceive the Zahir. According to the teaching of the Idealists the words 'live' and 'dream' are rigorously synonymous" (p. 164). In other words, the Zahir's replacement of the real world is equivalent to an idealistic—in Borges's work, in turn equivalent to imaginative—replacement of the real world. So the Zahir probably symbolizes the idealists' dream world or the imagination. The story's structure reinforces these last two themes, since the boxes both make the real world seem obscure and insubstantial and, since they are imaginative creations controlling the story, also make the imagination seem more powerful and real than reality.

Rather than stating his ideas directly, Borges communicates them by making a reader analyze these Chinese box systems. Gradually, as he does this, the reader discerns the premise on which Borges built them. Its relation to the story-within-a-story technique shows its debts to earlier literature that announced in muted tones its artifice. But the Literature of Exhaustion trumpets its artifice, elaborates this technique—though perspicaciously enough so as not to be merely gaudy but hollow—and cleverly relates this device to its themes.

A similar but less sophisticated device appears in Borges's work not as a way to put together a story but as a recurring idea, a thematic equivalent of the Chinese boxes. This is the *regressus in in-*

finitum, an infinite series, which Barth mentions in his essay on the Literature of Exhaustion and which a writer can use to open up an infinite number of possibilities. This idea usually appears in Borges's allusions, the most common one referring to Zeno's paradox of Achilles and the Tortoise. "Avatars of the Tortoise" starts with this story of the frustration of the hero who, although ten times faster than the tortoise, cannot catch it because it always runs a short distance while he makes up the distance it had just covered. Later in this story Borges describes other examples of the *regressus in infinitum.* He also likes to refer to Josiah Royce's map within a map within a map. . . . In "Time and J. W. Dunne" he says that Dunne "postulates that the future already exists and that we must move to it, but that postulate suffices to convert it into space and to require a second time . . . and then a third and a millionth" (*Other Inquisitions,* p. 20). In a more recent work, *The Book of Imaginary Beings,* Borges returns to this theme. In the article on Bahamut he recounts a Moslem cosmology that describes the earth resting on an angel that rests on a ruby and so on.

Borges's dependence on aesthetic subjects and techniques like the Chinese boxes and *regressus in infinitum* may make his work seem a bit limited and precious. Limited it is, but deliberately so, because he sees no value in many possible realistic topics which he deems inappropriate to literature. One should not call his work precious in a pejorative sense. He may work on a small canvas but he works on it exquisitely. The painter of miniatures does not necessarily have less skill than the titanic artist who covers entire walls. It may be useful to enumerate the kinds of subject matter Borges does not use and to explain his reasons for rejecting them or turning them to his own purposes. Then the area he has concerned himself with will stand out in sharper outline.

The topics he has avoided include nearly all the subject matter of realism. After even these few pages of exposition of Borges's work, it should be clear that he does not write in this mode. He usually points out his objections to realism with restraint and indirection. In a carefully embellished passage in "A Yellow Rose" he writes:

> Then the revelation occurred: Marino saw the rose as Adam might have seen it in Paradise, and he thought that the rose was to be found in its own eternity and not in his words; and that we may mention or allude to a thing, but not express it; and that the tall, proud volumes casting a golden shadow in a corner were not—as his vanity had dreamed—a mirror of the world, but rather one thing more added to the world. (*Dreamtigers*, p. 38)

He quarrels with realism primarily because it fails to recognize that, because words do not correspond exactly to the real world, a writer cannot connect with that world, so he would do better to pull in his borders and create a coherent, self-contained aesthetic artifact.

In "The Zahir" he makes the same point about realism even more indirectly with his description of language overcoming reality rather than mirroring it. Furthermore, earlier in this story Clementina Villar plays the role of a realistic writer, as indicated partly by a comparison of her and a major realist—"she was in search of the Absolute, like Flaubert"—and partly because of her behavior (*Labyrinths*, p. 157). She obsessively tries for absolute correctness in her dealings with the real world, but she inevitably fails because codes of behavior and styles, like language—as this story points out—are arbitrary and only tenuously related to reality. She finally loses because she decides to play on reality's grounds, where she inevitably will lose. First, she is embarrassed by being out of style; then, dying, the inevitable destiny of real people, she passes into an abstract world. The narrator remembers her as she was much earlier—changes her form by means of his imagination—just as he transforms inert objects: "the predictable rows of one- and two-story houses had taken on the abstract appearance that is theirs at night, when darkness and silence simplify them" (p. 158). After this the narrator immediately receives the zahir in his change, so then not only Clementina but also the whole universe can be dissolved.

Borges also rejects the realistic material that lies closest to a writer's hand: his own life. Some of his early poems do not conform to this generalization, but even they use autobiographical material in a peculiar way. Borges himself does not appear very often in them but he imbues them with his love of Buenos Aires—he called an early volume *Fervor of Buenos Aires*—and of Argentina. Martin Stabb quotes one of Borges's remarks from this period: " 'I believe that our verse should have a flavor of the *patria*, like a guitar that tastes of solitude, of the countryside and of sunset behind a field of clover.' "[8] Borges's work from the middle 1930s on, a period primarily of essays and fictions, is his important production, and this work is almost entirely nonautobiographical.

According to Borges, a writer should eschew autobiography because it is part of realism (which for him is prima facie evidence) and because during the act of writing the personality of the writer vanishes and a disembodied spirit replaces it. Borges described to Ronald Christ his collaboration with Bioy Casares under the pen name of H. Bustos Domecq: "we have somehow begotten a third person that is quite unlike us."[9] The same idea about the creative process lies behind the strange "Borges and I," in which he differentiates between himself as person and as writer: "I allow myself to live, so that Borges may contrive his literature" (*Dreamtigers*, p. 51). At the end of this work he does not know which of his selves wrote it, since in it he makes both a personal confession and a literary creation. In the opening of "The Zahir" he even proclaims his disbelief in the self's permanence. Because of its indirection and its occurrence amidst some fancy prestidigitation, critics often miss his most elaborate statement about the invalidity of even tenuously autobiographical literature. It appears in his first story, "Pierre Menard, Author of the *Quixote*," so he took his stand against autobiographical fiction as early as possible. He implies this stand by suggesting that another man can write, word for word, Cervantes's classic, which would make autobiography irrelevant to literature.

In regard to autobiography in his work, there remains to be dealt with the prickly problem of one of his most famous passages. It appears more than once, for instance at the end of *Dreamtigers'* epilogue:

> A man sets himself the task of portraying the world. Through the years he peoples a space with images of provinces, kingdoms, mountains, bays, ships, islands, fishes, rooms, instruments, stars, horses, and people. Shortly before his death, he discovers that that patient labyrinth of lines traces the image of his face.

Here he claims that a writer who thinks he has been describing the world has really been autobiographically describing himself. In other words, *realistic* writers merely reproduce themselves rather than creating something new. He does not say that all literature ultimately is autobiographical, but that realistic literature is futile. Very possibly he also means that a writer has no face—no personality —except his work.

The sociopolitical world does not interest Borges either. The malevolence of Peron and his shabby treatment of Borges, to whom he insultingly offered the post of Poultry Inspector for Fairs and Exhibitions, impelled Borges to write a one-page oblique attack on that dictator. "The Sham" (*Dreamtigers*, p. 31), however, is atypical of his work. A bit more often but still rarely he uses social or political material as he does in "Tlön, Uqbar, Orbis Tertius," in which he writes, "Ten years ago any symmetry with a semblance of order—dialectical materialism, anti-Semitism, Nazism—was sufficient to entrance the minds of men" (*Labyrinths*, p. 17). This statement sounds political, but the next sentence clarifies his purpose: "How could one do other than submit to Tlön, to the minute and vast evidence of an orderly planet?" He actually says that the desire for symmetry, and other mental failings, although lethal in the real world, harm no one in the world of imagination.

Borges also usually avoids psychology. Martin Stabb has found a revealing quotation on this subject in "Narrative Art and Magic," which, significantly, Borges wrote just before his earliest fictions. In it he denigrates the bulk of mid-nineteenth century fiction and its dominant "draggy novel of characters" and contrasts it with the ideal novel, "a precise game of staying on the alert, of echoes, and of affinities" (Stabb, p. 75). This attitude makes him almost completely avoid psychological themes and psychological analyses of his characters. Borges's characters perform peculiar, even outrageous, actions but rarely for any discernible motive. Extreme things happen to them but they remain stolid to the point of woodenness before them. Reading a Borges story, one feels like a baffled child watching lunatics; one does not empathize with the characters. Rather he watches Borges move them around as he would watch a Grand Master marshal the pieces on a chessboard.

Finally in regard to the subjects he avoids, Borges seems to have little interest in writing historical fiction. This does not mean that his work has no historical ingredients, only that in it he transforms history into an aesthetic construct. That is, according to him "it may be that universal history is the history of a handful of metaphors." This statement begins "The Fearful Sphere of Pascal," which sketches "a chapter of this history" (*Labyrinths*, p. 189). As if to prove this point he uses a few metaphors again and again in his work. He particularly enjoys mentioning the sphere whose circumference is nowhere and whose center is everywhere. He bases *The Book of Imaginary Beings*, seemingly a *jeu d'esprit*, on this view of history as well as on some of the other major principles of his work. A compendium, it presents an ahistorical survey of both Western and Eastern culture that endlessly elaborates a few metaphors. Like his bias against autobiographical literature, his bias against historical literature appears under the surface of "Pierre Menard, Author of the *Quixote*." This fiction implies that if a man living in a later century can exactly reproduce *Don Quixote*, the original version cannot have been linked in any way with its historical era. He attempts to discredit historical literature because he has a more pervasive antipathy: to time, the material of history.

After he dismisses all of these subjects, Borges has left little except aesthetic themes; his literature basically is about literature, a quality that links him with the Symbolists. Writers of this kind of literature build an artificial construct, rather than rendering in artistic form meaningful details from a meaning-laden world. Patricia Merivale has gone over this ground in her article "The Flaunting of Artifice in Vladimir Nabokov and Jorge Luis Borges," and in her title she has coined an apt term for this quality.[10] "The Library of Babel" contains Borges's most vivid exposition of the reason why he creates artificial literature primarily about literature. The library described in the story oppresses a viewer because of its regularity: made of hexagonal cubicles, and having five shelves on each wall, thirty-two books on each shelf, 410 pages in each book, forty lines on each page, eight letters in each line (*Ficciones*, p. 80). In this story the universe is a library, and the books, both individually and collectively, mean nothing substantive. The only meaning in the universe derives from its relentless order or, in other words, its artifice.

For example, Borges makes literature from literature by frequently modeling one work on another work. He considers acceptable this strategy and the use of allusions because they repeat earlier literature, whereas he considers memory harmful to writers because it repeats reality. Some of Borges's fictions, for instance "The End," obviously depend on the Argentine gaucho epic *Martin Fierro* by Hernández (*Ficciones*, pp. 159–162). In this fiction he invents a new destiny for two characters from that epic. Similarly, John Updike argues convincingly that "The Waiting" may be a gloss on Hemingway's "The Killers" (*Labyrinths*, pp. 165–168; Updike, p. 242). A piece of evidence supports Updike and weighs much in a Borgesian world: these two almost totally different authors were born in the same year, a trick of time that probably greatly amuses the Argentinian member of that pair. I would also argue that "The Secret Miracle" harks back to Ambrose Bierce's "Incident at Owl Creek Bridge" (*Labyrinths*, pp. 88–94). The apparent cessation of time in each is too similar to be coincidental.

Often he makes passing references to other works. His range of allusion, and therefore his erudition, staggers a reader; his references are not the sort one plucks from Bartlett's. For example, in one paragraph in which he lists comparisons between women and flowers he cites the Bible, the story of Math ("the fourth branch of the medieval Welsh tale known as the Mabinogion"), the *Nibelungenlied*, Ariosto (who was imitating Catullus), Tasso, Malherbe, Shakespeare, Swinburne, Stevenson, Milton, and Darío (these last two modestly tucked away in a footnote). After this display of knowledge, when he says, "this list might go on without end," one believes him.[11] The work already done on his allusions makes needless further discussion of that topic here. Ronald Christ's fine *The Narrow Act* covers this subject thoroughly, particularly when it explains Borges's debt to De Quincey. In *The Mythmaker* Carter Wheelock often forces his arguments, but sometimes he finds interesting analogies, such as those between Fitzgerald's translation of *The Rubaiyat* and some of Borges's works.[12]

Borges has also in other ways made literature from literature and from literary theory. In addition to his stories that use Chinese boxes, most of his fictions, and even more clearly his essays, belong in this category. Several critics have noticed this important feature of his work. In his series of interviews with Borges, Richard Burgin remarks, "You've really based your whole literature on literature itself in a way," and Borges concurs.[13] Updike again has a useful insight: "I feel in Borges a curious implication: . . . Literature . . . is now the only world capable of housing and sustaining new literature" (p. 245). This obvious point need not be belabored, but some of the more interesting examples of it should be cited. He has an unusual trick of writing reviews of imaginary books, which he does, for example, in "The Approach to Al-Mu'tasim" (*Ficciones*, pp. 37–43). This tactic suggests that the "real" aspect of books, their physical presence, does not matter.

The rich carpet of "Pierre Menard, Author of the *Quixote*" contains a figure relevant to this topic. A careful reader of Borges soon learns that he must do his homework to understand him, but that Borges always plays fair, for instance by concealing in allusions keys to his work, as he does in this fiction. He tells his reader that Menard reproduces "the ninth and thirty-eighth chapters of the first part of *Don Quixote* and a fragment of chapter twenty-two" (*Labyrinths*, p. 39). The ninth chapter mentions Cid Hamete Benegali, the Arab to whom Cervantes attributes *Don Quixote*, a strategy like some of those that the Literature of Exhaustion uses. The thirty-eighth chapter contains Quixote's disquisition on the relative merits of the arts and war, a piece of not very rigorous literary theory. Borges probably refers to the part of the twenty-second chapter that mentions a writer who imitates other writers. These sections of the *Quixote* are thus literature about literature, so this reference in "Pierre Menard" is literature about literature about literature. I can clip this series on one end by writing criticism about literature about literature about literature, but the possibility of a *regressus in infinitum* lies open on the other end. His work develops the theme of literature so extensively and in so many ways that the world begins to evaporate before a reader of his work and a book takes its place. This replacement, another of his favorite motifs, appears, for example, in "Fastitocalon" in *The Book of Imaginary Beings*.

Borges has been interested in myth nearly as long as he has been interested in its kinsman, literature. As a child he wrote his first "book," a ten-page handbook of Greek mythology. He says in the "Parable of Cervantes and Don Quixote": "myth is at the beginning of literature, and also at its end" (*Dreamtigers*, p. 42). But he uses this word in a distinctive way, to make the point that Cervantes composed *Don Quixote* from books about chivalry and that this book subsequently became material for present day writers, just as all literature goes through this same borrowing and lending process. He thus equates myth and the world of the imagination, of literature, not the world of archetypes or whatever. *The Book of Imaginary Beings* contains myth in this special sense, because Borges composed it from bits of earlier literature. However, it is not a handbook of mythology in the usual sense. Misinterpreting Borges's use of "myth" opens the door for fundamental misreading of his work. Ronald Christ usually writes circumspectly about myth in Borges's work. Wheelock in *The Mythmaker*, however, seriously distorts Borges by trying to prove that "the world in which Borges' fictive creations move about is a primeval world and has all the earmarks of the archaic cosmology" (p. 20). The little word "the" attached to "archaic cosmology" signals a big mistake, a frequent one of myth criticism: oversimplification or blurring of distinctions. He also makes the common errors of overextending his definition of myth so that it includes things that could more simply and convincingly be called something else, and of allegorizing details by lifting them out of their shimmering texture and cutting their ties to other details. These tactics usually cause a misreading and such turgidity and forced logic as: "the citizen attributes of Babylon [in "The Lottery of Babylon"] were complaining that they did not win in the lottery; that is, they were not being hypostatized by the ideational machine" (p. 117).

These aesthetic matters seem sombre, but Borges often treats them jocularly, because he at least considers the idea that literature is a game. This sword cuts two ways: it makes literature appear artificial and self-enclosed, to which he assents, but it also makes it appear nonserious, not in Huizinga's sense of creative playfulness but in the sense of frivolity. Borges captures the ambiguity of "game" in "For Bernard Shaw": "the concept of literature as a formal game leads, in the best of cases, to the good work of the period and the strophe, to a proper craftsman (Johnson, Renan, Flaubert), and in the worst of cases, to the vexations of a work formed of surprises dictated by vanity and chance (Gracián, Herrera Reissig)" (*Other Inquisitions*, p. 173). He plays in the positive sense of the word with the themes and techniques of the Literature of Exhaustion. He indicates only very rarely that this term has a negative sense. These few instances demonstrate his self-examination and his ability to see himself as some others see him. He can recognize the possible silliness of the literary life, as he reveals in "The Approach to Al-Mu'tasim." In a footnote to that fiction he parodies first the occasional pomposity of scholarship and then the possible crudity of folklore (*Ficciones*, p. 43). More direct self-scrutiny occurs in "An Examination of the Work of Herbert Quain." At times Quain seems very like Borges, and at one point Quain mentions his gamesmanship: " 'I lay claim in this novel . . . to the essential features of all games: symmetry, arbitrary rules, tedium' " (*Ficciones*, p. 75).

Thus, Borges understands the arguments against creating a highly aestheticized literature, of divorcing himself as completely as possible from the mundane world in order to try to make pure form. But he deems the dangers far less weighty than the rewards. And even though he occasionally watches and evaluates himself at work, checking his premises, he has for a long time rigorously adhered to his principles. A reader must meet him on these aesthetic grounds, not on the grounds of myth in the usual sense or on any nonliterary grounds like sociology.

In spite of his carefully limited subject matter, Borges does interesting things with genre, especially when he uses a reader's preconceptions about whether or not a certain genre usually is realistic. He does this to make the boundary between reality and imagination seem arbitrary, if not meaningless.

To be specific, in "Tlön, Uqbar, Orbis Tertius" he raises the problem of genre by imitating a genre. Although this is a work of fiction, references to Borges himself and Bioy Casares and the presence of apparent facts make it seem like an essay. An imaginary encyclopedia article, another genre, also plays an important part in the narrative. This imitation serves two purposes. First, it illustrates one sense of exhaustion by implying that the possibilities for original fiction have dried up so that a writer has no choice but to imitate other forms. Second, it tricks the reader by playing on his past reading experience. He expects the truth or at least the writer's version of it from an essay, and even more so from an encyclopedia. But a reader accustomed to opening his *Britannica* or a book of essays when he wants a fact will enter a phantasmagorical world when he opens the pages of "Tlön, Uqbar, Orbis Tertius." Most likely he will immediately wonder whether classifying works into genres will lead to real distinctions, and perhaps he will begin to doubt the reality of other categories.

In *The Book of Imaginary Beings*, too, Borges uses the reader's preconceptions about genre, though less cleverly, to shake the reader's confidence that he can distinguish reality from imaginative constructions. This book may seem like an introduction to animals or like excerpts from an encyclopedia, two forms that have a strong claim to being reports of reality. To the more skeptical reader this book may resemble a medieval bestiary, with one foot in primitive zoology and the other, because of its allegory, in ethics. Its title, though, suggests that it belongs entirely to the realm of the imagination, and it does describe a menagerie of bizarre animals, some charming because of their exoticism, others horrible because of their otherworldliness. He assembled this collection to cast doubt on these genres that writers supposedly use to describe the real world.

In "Tlön, Uqbar, Orbis Tertius" when the elements of fiction begin to break through the screen of the essay-like qualities one sees a mixture of genres, another of Borges's most common devices. Sometimes, following the lead of one of his favorite writers, Chesterton, he mixes them by adding a metaphysical overlay to a detective story. "Death and the Compass," for example, probably derives from Chesterton's Father Brown stories. Acknowledging Borges's mixing of genres, Martin Stabb in a long section of his book classifies Borges's fictions into three groups (pp. 94–136). One contains essayistic fiction (e.g., "Pierre Menard" and "Funes the Memorious"); another, intermediate fiction (e.g., "Tlön, Uqbar, Orbis Tertius" and "The Library of Babel"), and the last, short stories (e.g., "The Circular Ruins" and "Death and the Compass"). Although sometimes Stabb makes shrewd analyses, his classification, questionable from the beginning, breaks down when he discusses the works in these terms. For instance, although he calls "Funes the Memorious" essayistic fiction, he begins his account of it with a plot summary. This kind of classification seems futile and, more important, misguided. One must be careful to avoid arguing about which works of the imagination are most real; Borges tries to tell people that, to use Gilbert Ryle's term, that is a "category mistake."

Rather than classifying each of his works, it will be more useful to find a suitable label that fits them all and then, remembering Wittgenstein's insight, admit that these works have only a family resemblance. Paul de Man proposes a fairly suitable label: "the least inadequate literary analogy would be with the eighteenth-century *conte philosophique*: their world is the representation, not of an actual experience, but of an intellectual proposition." [14] His definition fits another term that describes a tradition both broader and richer than the *conte philosophique*. The works that Northrop Frye calls anatomies basically convey ideas rather than things, and they satirize pedantry while sometimes being guilty of it themselves. This description applies also to Borges's work. Despite the appropriateness of these two labels, one of his book titles, *Ficciones*, provides a better label, and it also suggests the modernity of his work. Calling each of his works "a fiction" instead of "fiction" conjures up memories of Wallace Stevens's use of the term for those works that organize experience for us and tell us what kind of world we are coping with. Although they solve it differently, Stevens and Borges share a sense of urgency about the problem of the relation between imagination and reality, so they can appropriately share the term "fiction."

This genre well suits a writer interested primarily in philosophical themes. Among his themes, one of the most important, both to his work and to the Literature of Exhaustion in general, is time. Borges has said, "I think that the central riddle, the central problem of metaphysics—let us call it thinking—is time." [15] In novels the appearance of this theme, even in exotic forms, surprises no one, since it traditionally has been one of the handful of dominant themes in that genre. Borges has never written a novel, but he retains his fascination for this topic. His interest in time does not contradict his antipathy toward realism because his treatment of this theme differs radically from most realists'. Realistic novelists usually consider time to be one of their most useful building blocks since it is a vital constituent of the real world they try to describe, but Borges, an anti-realist, argues against the existence of time. He vigorously attacks time, confident that the more he can discredit it, the more discredited will be reality and realism. Ana Maria Barrenechea correctly claims that in his work time is "one of those concepts which must be disintegrated in order to destroy the individual's awareness of himself as a real and self-contained entity" (p. 103).

Borges does not go unarmed into battle with time. He has read widely in philosophy, though he has chosen his reading to give himself not a conventional training in the history of philosophy but ideas for his writing. He believes that there is a clear-cut argument about this issue. His allies, the idealists, hold an anti-time position, whereas most other philosophers believe that time exists. In "A New Refutation of Time" he himself ventures onto the philosophical battleground to stand beside Berkeley and some of his other liege men like Hume and F. H. Bradley.

The battle between the pro-time and anti-time forces rages in fictional form within the imaginary kingdom of Tlön. Borges has foreordained the victor since Tlön is an imaginary, not a real, land and thus not dependent on time, and since Borges stages the battle. Adherents of one anti-time school in Tlön argue that time does not exist because "the present is indefinite, . . . the future has no reality other than as a present hope, . . . the past has no reality other than as a present memory" (*Labyrinths*, p. 10). Others claim that all time is past. On the opposite side, some vilified heretics argue for the existence of time by proposing a paradigm:

> On Tuesday, X crosses a deserted road and loses nine copper coins. On Thursday, Y finds in the road four coins, somewhat rusted by Wednesday's rain. On Friday, Z discovers three coins in the road. On Friday morning, X finds two coins in the corridor of his house. (p. 11)

This little story clearly suggests that a materialistic reality and time depend on each other for their existences.

A writer's ideas about time influence not only his themes but also the form of his works. Hladik, the main character in Borges's "The Secret Miracle," writes a play that begins by observing the unities, which of course means that it has a coherent time sequence. Factors in the story, such as the growing threat to Hladik by the Nazis, then begin to influence both the form and content of his play. Seven o'clock strikes twice, a sign of the time sequence's growing incoherence. Both Hladik and his main character, who, as it finally turns out, has imagined the whole play, change their allegiance from realism to idealism. As Hladik begins to accept idealistic theories of art, he becomes capable of performing the idealistic trick of stopping time for a year between his being shot and his death, so that he can finish his play. Hladik's play within the story, the narrative that frames it and comprises most of this fiction and, by implication, the fiction itself all suggest insistently that art can conquer time. In other words, Borges's theme is an ancient one, but he develops it after philosophy has dealt at length with time and after literature has got to the point where it may be close to exhaustion. Thus, "The Secret Miracle" more closely resembles one of Borges's favorite works, *The Thousand and One Nights,* than "Incident at Owl Creek Bridge." Borges adds an idealistic element to this much older work about a storyteller who uses art to defeat death by defeating time.

In "A New Refutation of Time" he reveals his two main strategies for his war against time: "the denial of time involves two negations: the negation of the succession of the terms of a series, negation of the synchronism of the terms in two different series" (*Labyrinths,* p. 232). He uses the second line of attack less often, probably because it has fewer possibilities for fiction, but he does use it in this same essay. He argues that in August, 1824, the battle of Junín took place in South America and De Quincey published an article in England. Since De Quincey and the captain who led the winning troops in the battle did not know each other, the two events, though apparently simultaneous, were not synchronous. Hence, time does not exist. Besides having little possibility for literature, this argument intrinsically does not compel assent.

The other strategy, although also somewhat dubious philosophically, forms an interesting basis for literature. Borges describes this strategy by putting it in the form of a question: "Is not one single repeated term sufficient to break down and confuse the series of time?" (p. 224). He begs the question, since the possibility of repetition depends on the existence of time. His premise, however, has possibilities for plot construction. In "The Cyclical Night" he asserts that terms indeed are repeated:

> They knew it, the fervent pupils of Pythagoras:
> that stars and men revolve in a cycle;
> the fateful atoms will bring back the vital
> gold Aphrodite, Thebans and agoras.
>
> In future epochs, the centaur will oppress
> with solid, uncleft hoof the breast of the Lapith;
> when Rome is dust, the Minotaur will groan
> once more in the endless dark of its stinking place.
>
> (*Personal Anthology*, p. 155)

He also puts this belief in repetition into fictional form, sometimes by attributing it to one of his characters, such as Hladik, in "The Secret Miracle" (*Labyrinths*, p. 90). Hladik appropriately states this idea because he can stop time. Erfjord in "Three Versions of Judas" also believes in repetition; in fact, he uses Hladik as a source. Sometimes Borges insinuates this idea more subtly into a fiction. He integrates the repetition of *Macbeth* and *Julius Caesar* more fully into the plot of "Theme of the Traitor and the Hero."

He reinforces these explicit statements that events recur and thereby refute time, sometimes by using sophisticated methods that readers may not even consciously notice, like the hidden refutation in "A New Refutation of Time." Borges drops a hint about this argument, and creates a contradiction he has to explain, by putting "new" in the title. However, he has slyly created a repetition by publishing two refutations of time, which also share some of the same arguments. The contradiction occurs because "new" implies the existence of time. The fact that most of his books are anthologies makes possible another kind of repetition; some of his works appear in more than one book, and works from more than one earlier book appear in later ones. *Labyrinths*, his most interesting collection, contains thirteen of the seventeen works from *Ficciones*, items from *Other Inquisitions* and *Dreamtigers* and some other works. And of course he repeats bits and pieces, sometimes from other writers, such as a list of people who have thought that there is an animal in the moon, and the references scattered throughout his work to the fearful sphere (*Book of Imaginary Beings*, p. 150). Sometimes he repeats more distinctive items, for example, the labyrinth image. His detractors objected as early as the 1940s that his repetitions vitiated his work, but such a charge is not necessarily valid, and Borges has a definite reason for repetition.

He borrows from Schopenhauer another argument against time that he uses in "A New Refutation": "No man has ever lived in the past, and none will live in the future; the *present* alone is the form of all life" (*Labyrinths*, p. 233). Again he tries to refute the sequential nature of time, the attribute on which he believes time depends. He usually develops this argument by showing that, at the moment of creation, an artist, by forming a timeless object, stops the intrusion of the future. Because he can create art, Hladik in "The Secret Miracle" can create a moment that, though not eternal, lasts for a year. In his own work Borges has created another bastion against time, a more impregnable one, not only because it contains Hladik's but also because it is more expertly fashioned than Hladik's. A tableau suitable to Borges's theories of time presents the aged Borges sitting quietly, in his blindness, composing fictions to prove that time cannot touch man.

But some of his characters have not learned this lesson. Dahlmann in "The South" shares with his creator some superficial resemblances, like an attack of septicemia caused by a blow to the head, but he believes in time. Neither the delirium caused by pain nor his copy of *The Thousand and One Nights* suggests to him that he, too, can escape from mundane existence through art. Instead he considers space to be a metaphor of time—which implies that he considers time to be real—and he goes southward, thus seeming to confirm his notion of time, for "it might have [almost certainly did] occurred to Dahlmann that he was traveling into the

t and not merely south" (*Ficciones*, p. 171). The narrator of
he Zahir" also converts time into space, his metaphor for time
ing money. Ironically, in these two instances neither character
ealizes that the ease with which he converts time into objects that
exist in space can be used as an argument that time has no existence
by itself.

Disliking time, Borges almost inevitably dislikes its storehouse,
memory. Both evils afflict the title character in "Funes the Memorious," which shows how they work in combination. Funes always
knows the time precisely without consulting a watch, but his remarkable ability does not please him: he tells others the time in a
shrill, mocking voice. Nor does anything else please him. He feels
oppressed and he lives like a prisoner, restrained physically by an
injury and restrained mentally by his constant awareness of time.
His other peculiarity, an unerring and all-encompassing memory,
burdens him even more. Remembrances pile up in his mind until
they leave no room for thought. He continually recalls things, shuf-
fles them by converting numbers into things, catalogues his memories. Despite the illusion of newness that these projects afford, he
merely repeats old things. This futility indicates memory's flaw;
rather than getting on with the task of creating infinite new possibilities, it repeats old ones. At last Funes fills with memories so
that he dies, appropriately of congestion. The manner of his death
states a warning about the unendurable pressure of memory.

In the same way that his memory torments Funes, the Zahir
torments the narrator of the story named for it. This character suffers from insomnia, which, according to Borges, symbolizes memory. The Zahir relates to these topics because Moslems believe
that it signifies "beings or things which possess the terrible property
of being unforgettable, and whose image finally drives one mad"
(*Labyrinths*, p. 161). Although he begins to live in an idealistic
dream world rather than the real world, the narrator does not become mad. Nevertheless this story states a powerful warning against
the perils of memory. Note, too, that he obsessively remembers a
coin, which earlier in the story represents time. When the narrator

actually experiences the Zahir instead of merely remembering it, however, it does not harm him after all, for it replaces the real world in his thoughts and thus can liberate him. By adding one more thing to the world, it offers a way to escape the limitations of the preexistent world.

Borges much less frequently disparages the other main constituent of the real world, space. He does, however, attack it in "The Zahir," using a clever two-part strategy. First, he reduces the world to a single thing. Then he obliterates that thing, thereby completely destroying the real world. In his *Paris Review* interview he hints that he learned this strategy from De Quincey, who wrote something to the effect that "everything in the world is a secret glass or secret mirror of the world" (p. 130). According to De Quincey, any object contains the world. Elsewhere Borges limits this property to peculiar objects like the fearful sphere of Pascal whose center is everywhere and whose circumference is nowhere. Occasionally Borges alters this image slightly; for example, the Library of Babel "is a sphere whose exact center is any one of its hexagons and whose circumference is inaccessible" (*Labyrinths*, p. 52). The Aleph in the story named for it also contains the entire universe:

> The Aleph's diameter must have been about two or three centimeters, but Cosmic Space was in it, without diminution of size. Each object (the mirror's glass, for instance) was infinite objects, for I clearly saw it from all points in the universe. (*Personal Anthology*, p. 150)

But reducing the world to one thing is only half the battle, and Carlos Argentino Daneri in "The Aleph" can go no further. He misses the hint about ways to take the second and final step. This hint lies buried in the seemingly ancillary information surrounding the story of the Aleph itself. Aside from the Aleph, the subjects in this story are mainly literary. Daneri writes a compendious work in the tradition of Michael Drayton's *Poly-Olbion* but his will include more, exhaustively describing not just England but all of the world. That is, he tries to bring realism to its pinnacle. However, he does not realize that he can solve his problem by creating non-realistic literature. He writes wretchedly, like an author who through a literary injustice won a prize deserved by Borges, but he wins a literary contest, and the narrator's work receives no votes. To compensate him for his lack of talent Daneri has the magical Aleph, but he lets it languish unused in his shabby cellar, and then he gives in to the narrator and allows his house to be torn down and, presumably, the Aleph to be destroyed. The realistic world, in the form of the gaudy confectionary that overruns his land, triumphs. This outcome justly punishes him for his failure to use the Aleph to destroy the real world.

The narrator of "The Aleph" almost finds a way to take the second step. He denies that Daneri's Aleph is the real one, and the story ends with this lament:

> Does that Aleph exist in the innermost recess of a stone? Did I see it when I saw all things, and have I forgotten it? Our minds are porous with forgetfulness; I myself am falsifying and losing, through the tragic erosion of the years, the features of Beatriz. (*Personal Anthology*, p. 154)

He has unwittingly answered his own questions. Beatriz, his dead loved one, is his Aleph; in a sense she comprises his world. She almost means to him what Beatrice means to Dante, but he has written *The Cards of the Cardsharp* instead of a work like *Vita Nuova* or *The Divine Comedy*, in which Dante transmutes a Beatrice, an Aleph, into art. Only creation of art, then, can disintegrate the one object to which the world has been reduced.

Borges distinguishes among kinds of patterns, some valuable and others valueless. He approves of purely aesthetic patterns clearly presented as such. For example, he favors a patterned prose style, and he certainly does not write chaotically and slovenly. He meticulously composes his burnished works. He also carefully orders the body of his work by discreetly using repetition to create patterns of thematic resonances. Borges makes his own patterns, but other writers mistakenly find patterns either in the world or in literary conventions. The realists sometimes see patterns that do not exist; for example, psychological writers presume to display the etiology of their characters' personalities. Traditionalists also err by selling themselves into bondage to literary conventions.

Borges's objection to patterns becomes clearer if one analyzes his references to a specific kind of pattern, symmetry. He disapproves of symmetry, first, because it is an important attribute of reality. In "The South" one learns that "reality favors symmetries and slight anachronisms" (*Ficciones*, (p. 169). Dahlmann in this story cannot free himself from reality, although reality's dependence on time, not symmetry, victimizes him. The main character of "Averroes' Search" also understands the connection between reality and symmetry: "the fear of the crassly infinite, of mere space, of mere matter, touched Averroes for an instant. He looked at the symmetrical garden; he felt aged, useless, unreal" (*Labyrinths*, p. 152). Averroes succeeds no better than Dahlmann in his dealings with the symmetrical world, since his attempt to explicate Aristotle —to live vicariously in another time—fails because he cannot fathom the alien Greek culture's drama.

Symmetry oppresses none of Borges's characters more than Erik Lönnrot in "Death and the Compass," who begins by worshipping it. This bookish detective sees a symmetrical pattern developing in a series of murders. Because the person who kills a delegate to a Talmudic conference leaves a note saying "the first letter of the Name has been uttered," Lönnrot anticipates three more murders to fill out the "name." He works out one symmetry by plotting the first three murders on a map and then adding the appropriate fourth point to the equilateral triangle. He deduces the day of the last murder by realizing that each of the first three happened on the third day of a month. When his vectors of space and time converge and he goes to apprehend the criminal, he confirms his reasoning based on symmetries: "the house of the villa of Triste-le-Roy abounded in pointless symmetries" (*Labyrinths*, p. 83). But the scenario of this drama of symmetries turns into an elaborate trap laid by his enemies. Basing their plans on Lönnrot's obsession with symmetry, they have brought him to their lair to kill him.

The geometry in "Death and the Compass" indicates that symmetry has other faults besides its association with reality. Borges uses an equilateral triangle to clarify his reasoning, almost as if he were drawing it on a blackboard. Lönnrot wants to add one more point and connect it with the triangle to create another symmetrical figure. He chooses to draw the point to the south of the original triangle, since the first three points were in the north, east and west of the city. He had two other possibilities that would have allowed him to make a symmetrical figure, points due east and west of the northern point of the triangle. In other words, one can complete a symmetry in only a finite—usually very small—number of ways. Therefore, one will soon exhaust its possibilities, which makes symmetry anathema to the Literature of Exhaustion.

Borges often signals his disapproval of people who believe in these negative themes. Such characters simply die. The villains kill Lönnrot, and Dahlmann in "The South" is about to die as the story ends because he has allowed himself to be drawn into a knife fight that he has no chance of winning. Borges's sturdy and persistent opposition to the limited and realistic themes of time, memory, space, and symmetry suggests that he just as strongly favors infinite and idealistic themes.

Borges sometimes settles for a less desirable goal than creating infinite literature based on the world view of idealism. He occasionally will use up a finite set of literary possibilities. This latter project accords with the present enervated state of fiction, and he always has a chance to turn a project of this kind into one with endless possibilities. The Histriones, a heretical sect in "The Theologians," have, like the writers they symbolize, got down to the business of exhaustion. They "reasoned that the world would end when the number of its possibilities were exhausted; since there can be no repetitions, the righteous should eliminate (commit) the most infamous acts, so that these will not soil the future and will hasten the coming of the kingdom of Jesus" (*Labyrinths*, p. 123).

The Histriones' project will end—they wish it to—but the Baby-

Ionians in "The Lottery in Babylon" have discovered that they can open up an infinitude of possibilities by using permutations and combinations. In their lottery *the number of drawings is infinite. No decision is final, all branch into others*" (*Labyrinths*, p. 34). Borges follows this same principal in *The Book of Imaginary Beings*. In its preface he states:

> Let us pass now from the zoo of reality to the zoo of mytholo-
> gies, to the zoo whose denizens are not lions but sphinxes and
> griffons and centaurs. The population of this second zoo
> should exceed by far the population of the first, since a mon-
> ster is no more than a combination of parts of real beings, and
> the possibilities of permutation border on the infinite. (p. 16)

In literature lie the vital possibilities for creating infinity, such as the principle Borges uses in *The Book of Imaginary Beings*. How-ever, he has better ways to accomplish his purpose than the strategy on which he bases this book. By multiplying language, especially on the minuscule scale of the letter, he can more efficiently produce an infinitude than he can by multiplying subject matter like the monsters. Borges gives credit for this insight to Kurd Lasswitz, who "toyed with the staggering fantasy of a universal library which would register all the variations of the twenty-odd orthographical sym-bols, in other words, all that it is given to express in all languages."[16] Borges of course toys with the same staggering fantasy in "The Library of Babel."

His many-pronged attack on realism and reality proceeds slowly against an implacable enemy. Sometimes he makes imaginative creations seem real, and reality seem imaginative. As an idealist, he feels justified in doing this. He told L. S. Dembo, "I wonder why a dream or an idea should be less real than this table for example" (p. 317). Besides the obvious source, Berkeley, the influence of Schopenhauer, especially his belief that the will produced the world, led Borges to this belief. A writer who accepts idealism gains pri-marily an increased number of possibilities for subject matter, since the imagination can create an infinity of objects. This motive lies just under the surface of a statement that Borges makes in a preface of *The Book of Imaginary Beings*: "The title of this book would justify the inclusion of Prince Hamlet, of the point, of the line, of the surface, of n-dimensional hyperplanes and hypervolumes, of all generic terms, and perhaps of each one of us and of the godhead. In brief, the sum of all things—the universe" (p. 13). Thus, the impossibility of distinguishing between the real and the imagined frees a writer from the realists' compunction to describe the world accurately, so he can write in any way he likes about anything.

Borges does not always try by discursive and straightforward means to force his readers to reconsider the boundary they have drawn between reality and the imagination. But at least once the magician does explain his trick by telling why he uses some of his favorite images. In the well named "Partial Magic in the *Quixote*" he writes:

> Why does it disturb us that the map be included in the map and the thousand and one nights in the book of the *Thousand and One Nights*? Why does it disturb us that Don Quixote be a reader of the *Quixote* and Hamlet a spectator of *Hamlet*? I believe I have found the reason: these inversions suggest that if the characters of a fictional work can be readers or spectators, we, its readers or spectators, can be fictitious. (*Labyrinths*, p. 196)

Working indirectly with these same devices in his fiction, and using them to involve the reader emotionally, he makes his philosophical theorizing seem to his reader not a trivial game, but a deadly serious endeavor.

In his fictions various kinds of imaginary constructs replace the world or part of the world. For instance, the lottery of Babylon starts on a small scale, but it gradually grows until it is the only reality in Babylon, or until Babylon has no reality. The citizens of Babylon are disturbed that this lottery has replaced their previous lives. They can neither escape nor control this seemingly omnipresent lottery that denies them all freedom of choice. Borges objects on simpler grounds: the lottery is not an aesthetic construct but a real one and therefore inherently unsatisfying. He also presents characters who act in a certain way because they are analogues of other literary characters. These cases appeal to Borges because they are literary. In these examples works of literature actually determine action that appears to be freely performed. Also in these examples the real world, according to the norms of the fictions, gives way to the imaginary world.

In "The Zahir" a partial replacement of reality precedes a total replacement. In the first step Clementina and the houses change from totally real to abstract (*Labyrinths*, p. 158). This change represents the creation of literature from its subject matter, as does the eventual replacement of the entire real world by the Zahir. At the very end of "The Zahir," during the account of the Sufis' repetition of names until they become meaningless, Borges more clearly identifies literature as the phenomenon that replaces the world. The Sufis' words, a product of their imagination and a primitive kind of literature, become the sum of the Sufis' reality.

Borges describes even more clearly the replacement of the world by literature in "The Library of Babel." The first phrase of this story suggests that books can replace the world, but the narrator doubts that this has happened: "the universe (which others call the Library)" (*Labyrinths*, p. 51). The narrator, however, seems gradually to be won over to the belief that books have supplanted reality as the basic constituent of the universe, for his speculations about the library begin to sound like attempts to formulate a cosmology. He considers the library's shape and order, whether it is infinite and eternal and contains a god, the role of chance in it and its meaning, if any. The library, of course, symbolizes literature.

The gradual ascendancy of literature over reality occurs also as "The Immortal" unfolds. In this fiction the characters change levels of being by imitating characters from other works of literature, and thereby they achieve immortality. The first to do so is Homer, who becomes the man called Argos, who in turn gets his name from a dog in *The Odyssey*. When Homer assumes this role he becomes unnervingly reticent, almost canine in his wordlessness, but later he reveals his human identity. Cartaphilus undergoes a much more complicated metamorphosis. His name—lover of paper—indicates that he turns into a literary creation. He begins as Marcus Rufus, who has left his Roman legion, deciding to stalk not barbarians but immortality. But after finding "Argos" during his search, he begins to change into Homer. As Borges mentions, Rufus quotes some Homeric passages early in the story-within-a-story that he tells (*Labyrinths*, p. 117). After Rufus becomes immortal, literally by drinking from a magical stream, symbolically by passing into the world of literature, he takes various forms. Some of these are Homeric: a chronicler of the adventures of Sinbad (an Odysseus-figure), a subscriber to Pope's *Iliad* (a copy of which, as Cartaphilus, he sells and into which he places his narrative), a friend of Giambattista Vico (who argued that Homer was a symbolic figure). Curiously enough, he seems to be Lord Jim when he drinks the water that releases him from immortality; at least he is sailing to Bombay on the *Patna* at the time. Finally he assumes a mortal identity, as Cartaphilus, and after he sells the *Iliad* he dies on Ios, where according to legend Homer was buried (the clue to this can be found in references to Pliny, who, though not in the passage cited, recounts this legend). Borges intersperses the Homeric allusions among others that provide hints about the kind of transformation that happens. One example will do, a reference to act 5 of *Back to Methuselah*, which takes place "as far as thought can reach" and is set amidst stately Greek columns, among which move characters dressed in Greek costumes. Creating the ambiance of Greek drama in a modern play implies that entering the immutable world of literature will enable one to escape time. This intricately plotted and highly allusive story has a very important but simple meaning: the world of literature can replace the world most people call real.

The same meaning inheres in "Parable of the Palace." Its creator told Richard Burgin that "it's a parable about art existing in its own plane but not being given to deal with reality. As far as I can recall it, if the poem is perfect then there's no need for the palace"

(p. 80). His interpretation makes a good deal of sense. A poet and an emperor go on a symbolic journey through the latter's imposing palace and grounds. They begin in an overwhelming but realistic setting and then pass into areas exotic almost to the point of being otherworldly, the journey symbolizing a mixture of the real and the imaginary. There "what was real would confound itself with what was dreamt or, rather, the real was one of the configurations of the dream" (*Personal Anthology*, p. 87). Later the poet recites a poem that captures every sumptuous detail of the emperor's domain. This creation puts the two men into the world of pure imagination, and the emperor realizes that his palace, now superfluous, will be replaced by the poem.

Borges frequently notes, always positively, the conjunction of dream and literature, which makes possible the replacement of reality by literature. In the interview with L. S. Dembo he claims that two of his works, "Episode of the Enemy" and "The Twilight of the Gods," give accounts of dreams, and he says that dreams differ very little from literature (p. 320). He puts this latter theory in poetic form in "The Other Tiger":

> In South America, I pursue and dream you,
> O tiger on the Ganges' banks.
> In my soul the afternoon grows wider and I reflect
> That the tiger invoked in my verse
> Is a ghost of a tiger, a symbol,
>
> (*Dreamtigers*, p. 70)

This image provides the title for the book in which it appears. However, in a companion essay, "Dreamtigers," he admits that dreams do not always perfectly capture their subject matter.

Dream and world will almost inevitably resemble each other in some ways, however, because the world, as well as literature, is a dream. Again *Dreamtigers* provides the best example of a concept related to dreams. "Everything and Nothing" opens with a Borgesian statement of the familiar idea that Shakespeare had "negative capability." Borges slightly exaggerates Keats's idea so that

Shakespeare seems to have been a dream mechanism encased in a body. The characteristic sudden twist at the work's end makes manifest the reason why Shakespeare's literary dreams were so attractive. God tells the dead Shakespeare, " 'neither am I one self; I dreamed the world as you dreamed your work, my Shakespeare, and among the shapes of my dream are you, who, like me, are many persons—and none' " (p. 47). In "Avatars of the Tortoise" Borges claims that not God as he is commonly thought of but "the un-divided divinity that operates within us" has dreamed the world (*Other Inquisitions*, p. 120).

In the most famous of Borges's dream fictions, "The Circular Ruins," a hero goes to a ruined temple and begins slowly, meticu-lously to dream a man. When he succeeds, the man he has dreamed apparently becomes a part of reality, but soon the dreamer realizes that that is a dubious honor because he himself has been dreamed by another person. This story offers more than a shrewd preparation for a trick ending. The circularity of the ruins, undoubtedly impor-tant because Borges mentions it in the title, provides a hint as to this fiction's basic meaning. Like the fearful sphere in its circularity and its status as the only obviously real thing in the universe, this ruin represents infinity. The plot of this fiction represents the same thing because the dreamer dreaming a dreamer begins an infinite regress. Thus, these devices demonstrate a now familiar point: literature dependent on dreams has more possibilities than litera-ture dependent on reality, and perhaps its possibilities are unlimited. This meaning in turn suggests the premise on which Borges bases his development of the topic of dreams: dream, world, and litera-ture ultimately merge into one entity.

This premise typifies idealism, a philosophy that has been hinted at by Borges's development of some of the themes already discussed. His debts to Berkeley, Bradley, Schopenhauer, and other thinkers in this tradition should also be clear by now. Also, Jaime Alazraki points out the influence of *The Kabbalah* on the dream motif in "The Circular Ruins." [17] Borges makes somewhat less clear his debt to another idealist who influenced him. This appears in "Tlön,

Uqbar, Orbis Tertius," probably his most famous idealist fiction. Tlön's literature resembles a category defined by Meinong, who Borges mentions in this work. He divided objects into three categories: those that exist ("sein"); those that subsist ("sosein"), that is, could exist; and those that cannot exist. This grouping suggests another way of describing the idealist writer's advantage over the realist. The former can create objects that fall into the last two of Meinong's categories; the latter can imitate only objects in the first category.

L. S. Dembo makes another interesting point about the idealism in this story: "the philosophy of idealism prevalent on the imaginary planet Tlön seems to be vindicated when the actual world begins to transform itself in Tlön's image" (p. 316). Dembo refers to the appearance in the "real" world of several objects that the encyclopedists mentioned in their account of Tlön. Borges, too, would undoubtedly like to have some of his imaginary creations appear in the world outside his books. If this happened, it would mean that he had destroyed the border between reality and imagination, which in turn would be the end of realism and the ascendance of Borges's idealism.

The other main ideas that Borges approves have less, or no, connection with idealism. One of the most peculiar notions he toys with is that only one man exists in the world, and he is all men. He states this succinctly in "The Immortal": "one single immortal man is all men" (*Labyrinths*, p. 115). In his catalogues of various men who have held ideas in common Borges hints at the similarity of several men, a less extreme version of this idea. These catalogues also apply this idea to the realm in which it becomes meaningful for Borges, literature. He most fully develops the relation between this theme and literature by quoting Emerson in "The Flower of Coleridge": " 'I am very much struck in literature by the appearance that one person wrote all the books' " (*Other Inquisitions*, p. 9). He uses this idea, too, against realism, for a world populated by only one man hardly suits the concept of identity, which is important to the realists' world-view. The belief that there is only one author contradicts another premise of realism, that persons with definite identities living in definite times and places wrote each work of literature.

Borges aims secretly at realism as he develops his theme of the relation between language and reality. Realism partly depends on the belief that language can mirror reality, but he will not accept this belief. At least he disputes it in regard to the language of men. The narrator of "The God's Script" considers that "in the language of a god every word would enunciate that infinite concatenation of facts" (*Labyrinths*, p. 171). But man falls far short of this ideal; he cannot capture the concatenation of the universe in many words, much less in one. Man sometimes finds instead that his words have only the barest purchase on things, or no purchase at all. Borges delights in setting down histories of words to show this, like one in "The Zahir":

> In Guzerat, towards the end of the eighteenth century, the Zahir was a tiger; in Java, a blind man from the Mosque of Surakarta whom the Faithful pelted with stones; in Persia, an astrolabe. . . . (*Labyrinths*, p. 156)

This list, which contains a few more items, has a fanciful air, but he provides a credible history of "panther" in *The Book of Imaginary Beings*. He says that "in the Anglo-Saxon bestiary of the *Exeter Book*, the Panther is a gentle, solitary beast" (p. 178). If the meanings of words constantly change, in many of the instances—perhaps in all but one—they will not describe present reality.

Words can also be too powerful for the realist, altering reality instead of reporting on it. In "The God's Script" Borges mentions a combination of fourteen words that make whoever utters them omnipotent. Words can further confound realists by adding to reality. A combination of letters created one of the imaginary beings, the Golem (p. 112). In "The Library of Babel" Borges describes the utmost power of words. Here words have completely taken over the universe. These attributes of language frustrate the realist but delight the idealist, because, like many of the other ideas Borges favors, they create a myriad of possibilities.

These last few themes help make Borges's fictional world insubstantial and Protean. He usually subordinates the theme of metamorphosis to other themes like idealism or dreams, but once in a while it appears independently. The Baldanders in *The Book of Imaginary Beings,* creatures in German mythology, continually change their form; hence their name, which means "soon another." They resemble Proteus, but otherwise Borges is little interested in Ovid's gallery of metamorphosing creatures. Rather than describing a creature taking on a different guise within the realm of reality, Borges describes creatures who pass from reality to imagination or vice versa, keeping their identity. An example occurs in "The Immortal," where literary characters appear in the realm that, according to the story, is real. One would expect Borges to be more interested in metamorphosis, since Ovid's phantasmagorical world differs greatly from the usual conceptions of reality.

Borges considers the world to be in a constant flux rather than fixed for eternity. This notion would meet with little argument, but his process theory of art is more controversial. On this matter he seems Romantic, emphasizing the process of creating art, rather than the completed product, in order to glorify the mind that created art. Process intrigued the Romantics because of their adulation of inspiration, but Borges has more complicated reasons for emphasizing process, as this examination of his themes should indicate. His world constantly changes because the unreality of the "real" world forces him continually to create his own world of art. The alternative emphasis on product, a Classical position, binds writers to traditional rules of composition and forces them carefully to imitate "real" objects. Both rules and imitation repel Borges. His position on these questions appears in "The Secret Miracle." As long as Hladik continues to tinker with his play, to keep writing it, he remains alive. When a product issues from the process he dies.

Although Borges sometimes presents his ideas discursively, even in his fictions, he also frequently develops them by means of images. Besides varying his presentation, this imagistic method, especially in the case of his major images, gives him another way to achieve repetition and thereby attack time. Ana Maria Barrenechea and other critics have considered in detail some of his images, so I will pause for analysis of only three. The labyrinth, the mirror, and the circle are his most important images and also the most closely related to the Literature of Exhaustion.

The labyrinth's complexity results partly from its inherent nature and partly from the frequency with which this image occurs. This complexity makes it necessary to examine it in a large number of contexts. By understanding the labyrinth one can understand much of Borges's art. Appropriately, something that has a hidden answer itself reveals the hidden answer to his work, this condition being a Borgesian *regressus in infinitum*. Most critics have been unable to operate convincingly in the face of these difficulties; they see only one facet of this many-faceted image. Most of them focus on the negative aspects of the labyrinth. H. E. Lewald claims that "the symbolism inherent in the labyrinth represents first of all an irrational universe whose multiplicity, or unknown factors, exemplifies a lack of order or apparent purpose."[18] Leonard Murillo calls the labyrinth a "symbol of man's insecurity."[19] Borges himself has spoken about this aspect of the labyrinth: "it's the most obvious symbol of feeling puzzled and baffled, isn't it?"[20]

Although these two critics and Borges agree, they describe only a part of a part of the image. For one thing, their comments are limited to the labyrinth's role as a symbol of the world's chaos. If it meant only this, it would be a banal image, its banality multiplied by each appearance. Typically, Borges also adds an aesthetic dimension to this image's meaning. Realism's invalidity follows as a corollary from the theorem that the world is labyrinthine. Carter Wheelock senses this, for in his discussion of "The House of Asterion" he says that the minotaur represents the "idealist consciousness" living in the conceptual universe, which it projects (p. 27). He is on the right track, but his analysis breaks down when one

considers the details of the image. It makes little sense to imagine a
hero wandering through a maze to find and kill the idealist consciousness, which Borges certainly does not consider to be an enemy.
In short, Wheelock has generalized too hastily. It would be better
to say that the labyrinth itself has negative features in so far as it
represents reality.

But the labyrinth also has a positive side because of its connection
with the Literature of Exhaustion. One's guide to this aspect of it
must be John Barth, since he seems to be the only critic who has
recognized it. He understands this image more fully than other
critics because he places it in its proper context instead of looking
at it in isolation. He sees, as no one else does, that a person in a
labyrinth must exhaust all possibilities of choice (of direction) before he can reach its center (p. 34). In other words, one response
to the depletion of literature, though still not the best, is to write
so as to exhaust all the possibilities presented to one. In this light,
the labyrinth appears positive, because successfully dealing with it
symbolizes a valuable literary goal. This feature makes up for some
of the frustration in store for everyone who tries to work his way
through the labyrinth of the world.

So far, the key to understanding the image of the labyrinth has
been to see its artistic implications. The importance of the aesthetic
themes in Borges's work should make this an obvious strategy for
interpreters of his work. Furthermore, his references to labyrinths
include plenty of hints that this is the proper context for the image.
In "The Garden of the Forking Paths" one learns that "the book
and the maze were one and the same thing" (*Labyrinths*, p. 25).
Only one character, and only after a long time, recognizes that the
book—a novel by a Chinese author—is identical with the maze. In
"The Secret Miracle" Borges calls Hladik's play "his lofty, invisible
labyrinth" (*Labyrinths*, p. 94). Both books are related to time, the
Oriental one being "an invisible labyrinth of time," which makes
them limited and too realistic (p. 25).

The center of the labyrinth, the goal for which the hero endures the almost endless wrong turns, represents a better way to create literature. Critics who discuss only the labyrinth's negative aspect have not seen this goal. Sheer luck cannot be depended upon to find the center, and the exhaustion of possibilities constitutes only a holding action till a better way is found. No, one should expect the labyrinth to have a secret key. The ubiquity of this secret key theme in Borges's work contributes another vital clue to the meaning of the labyrinth, and again most of the critics have missed it. Martin Stabb sees the connection between this theme and the labyrinth, but he focuses his attention on the former: "The idea of the "hidden key" to a problem, the familiar labyrinthine view of the world, and the theme of an all-knowing divinity who seems only slightly concerned with man's attempts to solve eternal riddles, are, of course, notions which figure prominently in much of Borges' prose" (p. 50). Similarly, Ronald Christ recognizes that although labyrinths confuse people who view them from ground level, those who look down on them easily see their secret (p. 172). The many references to the word or sentence that contains the universe, to the Zahir and to the secret that the universe is really a dream support Stabb's and Christ's point that the labyrinth has a solution. The major sources of Borges's references to secret keys are Gnosticism and *The Kabbala*, arcana that fascinate him.

This idea of the secret key, too, must be applied to literature. Barth has also taken this step in the chain of reasoning that clarifies the labyrinth's meaning. He points out that the help Theseus had, especially from Ariadne, allowed him to avoid the difficulties of the maze. This alleviation of Theseus' task should remind writers not to waste their time and try their nerves by either describing or exhausting the labyrinth. It is much easier to write about the necessity of finding one's way through the labyrinth without actually making the trip. This abstruse idea becomes clearer if one remembers that the Literature of Exhaustion produces fresh work by pretending that literature is depleted and by using this situation as material, rather than facing the depletion directly. More specifically, Barth points out that Borges need not actually write the encyclopedia of Tlön; he merely has to state the idea. The hidden key, then, is to make labyrinths instead of trying to solve them.

At the center of the labyrinth stands the minotaur. In his article on it in *The Book of Imaginary Beings* Borges writes, "it is equally fitting that in the center of a monstrous house there be a monstrous inhabitant" (p. 158). The narrator of "The House of Asterion," a minotaur, derives much of his terror from his Philistinism, which is a valuable clue. Not realizing the contradiction he creates by speaking his opinions as the narrator of a story, he claims that "nothing is communicable by the art of writing" (*Labyrinths*, p. 139). The writer-hero must prove the minotaur wrong by communicating through writing. To paraphrase Barth, a writer can understand labyrinths and innovative literary movements like the Literature of Exhaustion, but he still must defeat the minotaur and get back out. That is, he must turn his insights into first-rate literature (p. 34).

Finally some of Borges's characters escape from the maze. In "The Immortals" the narrator manages an "ascension from the blind region of dark interwoven labyrinths into the resplendent City" (*Labyrinths*, p. 110). In addition to the splendor, a writer who has come this far attains immortality (at least in the form of immutable literature). This same story usefully recapitulates the meaning of the labyrinth: "there were nine doors in this cellar; eight led to a labyrinth that treacherously returned to the same chamber; the ninth (through another labyrinth) led to a second circular chamber equal to the first" (p. 109). The outer labyrinth represents the negative aspect of this image; the inner labyrinth represents the positive aspect. The outer labyrinth is also equivalent to the world, the inner to the labyrinthine structure erected by a writer who, fathoming the true state of the world and literature, uses for his own benefit the same kind of structure that has foiled other writers.

In Borges's work the mirror contrasts with the labyrinth. If the latter represents the Literature of Exhaustion, the former represents realism. The mirror naturally symbolizes realism since it imitates existing objects, as eighteenth century literary theory indicates. Borges states the contrast between mirrors and labyrinths (in this case, a labyrinthine book) in the first sentence of "Tlön, Uqbar, Orbis Tertius," which also is the first sentence of both *Ficciones* and *Labyrinths*: "I owe the discovery of Uqbar to the conjunction of a mirror and an encyclopedia." The hunt for the source of a quotation about a mirror energizes this story's plot. The quotation whose source the characters seek indicates that mirrors are negative: "For one of those gnostics, the visible universe was an illusion or (more precisely) a sophism. Mirrors and fatherhood are abominable because they multiply and disseminate that universe" (*Labyrinths*, p. 4).

Imitation of reality, although not intrinsically bad, creates a merely finite process because the objects it imitates are finite in number, as Marino in "A Yellow Rose" realizes. Despite his reputation as a writer worthy of comparison to Homer and Dante, he does not realize till the eve of his death that his books "are not a mirror of the world, but rather one thing more added to the world" (*Dreamtigers*, p. 38). This fact about his works is clearly positive, since Marino grasps it in an almost mystical experience—which is described by means of a conventional mystical symbol, the rose—and since the second comparison, at his death, of him to Dante and Homer makes this death seem like an apotheosis. He has grandeur because he breaks through the numerical limits of the things in the world, something a realist cannot do except in a very limited way, by creating a book. Unfortunately, he did not realize while he wrote what effect he was producing. If he had, he may have been worthy of comparison to Homer and Dante. The finite mirrors in "The Library of Babel" contrast with the library, which, as a fictive and idealist creation, is infinite.

To Borges, even when he was a child, mirrors meant the same thing they mean to him now, and they caused the same fear, as he told Richard Burgin (p. 16). In a disconcerting essay, "The Draped Mirrors," he confirms this: "as a child, I felt before large mirrors that same horror of a spectral duplication or multiplication of reality"

(*Dreamtigers*, p. 27). Perhaps the young Borges also spurned the mirroring of reality in the realistic works in his father's fine English library. It also would be interesting to know how he would have reacted as a child to a fairytale-like story about mirrors, "Fauna of Mirrors," that he tells in *The Book of Imaginary Beings*. In it the mirror-people are banished to their mirrors and forced to repeat the actions of men because of their invasions of the human kingdom, with which they had previously lived in harmony despite their differences. The storyteller predicts that the Fish will be the first of the mirror-people to give up this mimetic function. If so, they will become like writers of the Literature of Exhaustion.

The complications of Borges's circle imagery arise chiefly because he uses it both to attack the realists and to defend his own kind of literature. That is, like his labyrinths, his circles sometimes are positive, sometimes negative. Two discordant properties of circles cause this ambiguity when he relates them to literature. A circle shares with the kind of art he favors its virtue of self-containment. But if one imagines either the circle moving or someone moving around it, the starting point will eventually be reached again, making it repetitious and finite, like realism and other depleted types of literature.

The essay on the Uroboros in *The Book of Imaginary Beings* lists objects whose circularity represents infinity: the Greek conception of the ocean, the world-circling serpent, etc. Borges uses a circle in "The God's Script" to describe a mystical union with the divinity. The wheel that appears during that union is everywhere at once and infinite and contains opposites. A third positive use of the circle image occurs in "The Circular Ruins," where Borges connects it with idealism because the main character goes to a circular ruin to dream a man. This last example refers to a self-enclosed dream world that the real world cannot touch. In Borges's work infinity, timelessness and dreamlikeness are all qualities of the same type of art. In "The Circular Ruins" Borges adds a variation to his circle imagery. When the dreamer learns that he, too, is dreamed, one can picture the situation as a circle within a circle, perhaps ad infinitum.

This last phenomenon, oddly, appears also in one of the negative uses of the circle image. The outer circle in "The Secret Miracle" is Hladik's circular delirium; the inner circle is his play. The play's repetition makes it negative. The seven gongs of the clock, the light from the setting sun, the Hungarian music and the words that open the play are repeated at its end. Thus, the error of Hladik that leads to his death, finishing the play, like so many of the details in Borges's fiction, can be put meaningfully into an aesthetic context. Hladik's error shows that art must not be circular or otherwise finite. The circle as a symbol of finitude occurs also in "The Theologians." A heretical sect, the Monotones, believes that history is circular, a belief that two repetitions in the story partly justify. One theologian inadvertently writes some words written previously by another theologian. This leads to the second one's death as a heretic, and the first one dies in a similar way, though not for heresy. In short, this first repetition leads to death, and the second is a death.

The labyrinth, mirror, and circle images seem to have a good deal in common, and so do, on a smaller scale, Borges's less important images. One can decipher his very complex images only by analyzing the relation of the same image to various contexts. Often a single image will relate to several themes, which compounds the complexity. For this reason some of the more meaningful passages in his work need to be analyzed over and over from different viewpoints. All this makes his images sound coldly philosophical but many of them are laden with emotion. The circular ruins are unnerving, the stone mirrors in Adrogué melancholy and vaguely threatening, the labyrinths in the city of the Immortals oppressive and ominous. And all of his images do not evoke negative responses. Some are lovely, others charming and fascinating. He probably developed his skill with images during his apprenticeship as an Ultraist poet.

Some of Borges's themes and the limitations he imposes on his subject matter help shape his characters. His lack of interest in psychology, it will be recalled, makes most of his characters two-dimensional. He says, with some accuracy, "I'm afraid there are no characters in my work. I'm afraid *I'm* the only character."[21] His interest in philosophical topics accounts for the large number of intellectuals in his work, and his aesthetic interests call for many readers and writers. This by no means implies that he has created a gallery of forgettable characters. He vividly etches many of them in his reader's memory: Mad Herbert Quain, unhappy Funes, meticulous Erik Lönnrot, noble Emma Zunz, frustrated Averroes and a multitude of others.

Among his most significant characters are the doubles. The essay on the double in *The Book of Imaginary Beings* sketches in the background of these characters and gives many examples, both legendary and literary. Among the inspirations he mentions for the concept is one of his own favorite images, the mirror. His own doubles, however, differ from most other doubles in literature because he creates them to make a metaphysical, and ultimately an aesthetic, point rather than a moral point. That is, he uses doubles to refute the belief that people have clearly defined identities, a major premise of realism. His three most important doubles are composed of a murderer and a victim.

One pair of doubles appears in "The Waiting," because the victim takes the name of his pursuer, Villari. To recognize Aurelian and John of Pannonia in "The Theologians" as doubles, one must catch the significance of Aurelian's repetition of some of John's words and of his death. Aurelian indirectly kills John because his accusation of heresy leads to John's death. Erik Lönnrot, the detective, and Red Scharlach, the criminal, in "Death and the Compass" clearly are, respectively, victim and murderer, but only their names indicate that they are doubles. Because *scharlach* is German for "scarlet," *rot* is German for "red" and *Erik* almost invariably suggests "the Red," their names become Red Red and Red Red.

Borges makes a more surprising and determined attack by means of characterization on the concept of identity when he suggests that a person has a self only as long as he creates a fictive world. This holds true for Averroes in "Averroes' Search." He immediately disappears after it becomes apparent that he cannot reconstruct in his imagination Aristotle's world so that he will be able to comprehend the meaning of comedy and tragedy. The epilogue emphasizes this failure of Averroes by pointing out the similarities between Borges's task of recreating Averroes, a writer in an alien culture, and Averroes's attempted recreation of Aristotle. Borges also points out another infinite regress: "my narration was a symbol of the man I was as I wrote it and . . . in order to compose that narration, I had to be that man and, in order to be that man, I had to compose that narration, and so on to infinity." (*Labyrinths*, p. 155). This passage also helps clarify the enigmatic passage about the writer who "shortly before his death . . . discovers that that patient labyrinth of lines traces the image of his face" (*Dreamtigers*, p. 93). It suggests that writers, too, exist only when they are creating a fictive world, which is another reason to believe that the passage in *Dreamtigers*, supports idealism, not realism.

In "The Waiting" he creates an even more bizarre situation, for the fictive world that the character makes contains himself, and Borges describes the process step by step. At first, the central character seems real and distinct, although he takes the name of his pursuer. He goes to gangster films but "the idea of a coincidence between art and reality was alien to him (*Labyrinths*, p. 166), It does not remain alien for long, though, because when he reads *The Divine Comedy* he considers himself a character in a book: he "did not think Dante would have condemned him to the last circle, where Ugolino's teeth endlessly gnaw Ruggieri's neck" (p. 168). Finally, he repeats Ole Andresen in "The Killers," as Updike points out. This action turns him into another fictive character, so he has gradually created a fictive world with himself at the center. If selfhood depends on a fictive world, this buttress of a realistic world view will soon crumble.

One inspiration for Borges's attack on identity may be the folktales he records in *The Book of Imaginary Beings*, which show the falsity of even the broad categories of animal, vegetable, and mineral. The barometz is a "vegetable Lamb of Tartary," a plant shaped like a lamb, and the carbuncle is an animal with a precious stone in its head. Hume probably gave some of these ideas to Borges. In "New Refutation of Time" Borges describes Hume's position thus: "Hume did not wish us to add the metaphysical notion of a self to the succession of mental states" (*Other Inquisitions*, p. 193).

Although he writes very brief works—the longest of the *Ficciones*, "Tlön, Uqbar, Orbis Tertius," is only twenty pages long—his plots are worth discussing. One would expect them to be either like the plots of short stories, with an inexorable chain of events leading to a climax, or meandering like those of sketches. They are neither. Borges even orders, in an eccentric way, a long work with homogeneous subject matter and some claim to unity: *The Book of Imaginary Beings*. He arranges the beings in alphabetical order, but he does so idiosyncratically. For example, he puts "An Animal Imagined by C. S. Lewis" in the "A's" and "A Creature Imagined by C. S. Lewis" in the "C's."

Borges's most exotic idea for a plot is attributed to an imaginary writer, Herbert Quain, in "An Examination of the Work of Herbert Quain." Quain writes a novel with thirteen chapters, the first describing a dialogue, the next three describing possible eves to the day of the dialogue. Chapters five, six, and seven are possible eves to the night in chapter two; eight, nine, and ten possible eves to the night in chapter three; and eleven, twelve, and thirteen possible eves for the night in chapter four (*Ficciones*, p. 75). Because of these combinations, the novel actually is nine different novels. Borges has not tried anything like this; as Barth says, he need only imagine the possibility. Some of his endings, however, surprise readers, like the revelation that the dreamer is dreamed in "The Circular Ruins" and the self-identification of the narrator in "The Shape of the Sword." Borges always plays fair; a reader can see clues to the ending if he goes back over the story. Also, as with detective stories, the more of Borges's work one reads the more likely he is to anticipate the ending.

He also fills his work with coincidences. For instance, the spy in "The Garden of the Forking Paths," who searches for any person named Albert, finds one who has been fascinated by an ancestor of the spy. In regard to this subject, Borges remarked to Richard Burgin, "perhaps coincidences are given to us that would involve the idea of a secret plan" (p. 110). The crucial word in this statement, "secret," suggests that coincidences in life result from an order outside the cause and effect relationships that seem to control the real world. When they appear in literature coincidences suggest that logical patterns are not inherent in the world, waiting to be discovered by writers, but that a writer imposes them. A writer of the Literature of Exhaustion wants to force exactly this conclusion. Since a plot is a temporal order, disjointed plots also cast doubt on time. As Borges has said in "New Refutation of Time," one can attack time by showing that events do not connect in a time sequence. In summary, his use of plots supports his argument that our world lacks order and results from chance, that it is really a "lottery of Babylon."

Borges's masterful style can be appreciated even in translation, because its classical flavor makes it fairly easy to translate and because he, fluent since childhood in English, has supervised many of the translations of his work. A full analysis of his style would require working in Spanish, however, and would also wander far from the topic of this book. More useful here will be a few careful generalizations, which will reveal a change in his style that occurred as he changed from a literature that tries to exhaust possibilities to a more advanced form of the Literature of Exhaustion.

Early in his career, like many writers he wrote Baroque prose. In the prologue to an early book, *Universal History of Infamy*, he applies this term to his writing and defines it as "the style that deliberately exhausts (or tries to exhaust) all its possibilites." [22] In other words, early in his career Borges wrote like his narrator in "Tlön, Uqbar, Orbis Tertius," who goes on "revising, in the still days at the Adrogué hotel, an uncertain Quevedian translation (which [he does] not intend to publish) of Browne's *Urn Burial*"

(*Labyrinths*, p. 18). Borges greatly admires the two Baroque stylists mentioned, particularly the Englishman, and the aesthete he describes, living in his private world of style, probably was to Borges at one time an attractive portrait of the artist.

Later in his career, however, the principles of Ultraism that had shaped his early poetry seem to have begun to influence his prose. Stabb paraphrases these principles as they are stated in Borges's "Ultraist Manifesto": "the reduction of lyricism to metaphor; the combining of several images in one; and the elimination of adornments, sermonizing, and all forms of poetic filler" (p. 30).

By 1967 Borges had accepted this last, anti-Baroque principle thoroughly enough to announce, to a *Paris Review* interviewer, that he writes a classical prose:

Interviewer: You've worked, then, toward a kind of classical prose?
Borges: Yes, I do my best now. . . . If you write an uncouth word or an astonishing or an archaic word then the rule is broken; and what is far more important, the attention of the reader is distracted by the word. (148)

The sparseness that he advocates suits an author who uses the hypothesis that literature is exhausted. Also, it contrasts with his erudition and immense vocabulary to create an eerie tension.

Sparse though it is, his style certainly does not bore a reader, nor does he completely avoid astonishing words. For example, "The Circular Ruins" opens with a surprising combination of adjective and noun: "the unanimous night" (*Labyrinths*, p. 45). This strangeness is not created by the translation, which is literal: the Spanish is *"la unanime noche."* Strange words and passages like this one effectively lend an air of unreality to his work, which accords well with his theory of literature. And so his style, besides being pleasing in itself, reinforces the other elements of his work.

His tone deserves a brief commentary, if only to show that he is not overly-solemn. His mockery of the real world often engenders comedy, as do his weird characters and the abrupt turnings of his plots. The best examples are academic humor, which unnerve an academic critic of Borges. Knowing that one man's joke is another man's bore, I offer this tongue-in-cheek bibliography from "Pierre Menard, Author of the *Quixote*":

> p) An invective against Paul Valéry, in the *Papers for the Suppression of Reality* of Jacques Reboul. (This invective, we might say parenthetically, is the exact opposite of his true opinion of Valéry. The latter understood it as such and their old friendship was not endangered.)

> q) A "definition" of the Countess de Bagnoregio, in the "victorious volume"—the locution is Gabriele d'Annunzio's, another of its collaborators—published annually by this lady to rectify the inevitable falsifications of journalists and to present "to the world and to Italy" an authentic image of her person, so often exposed (by very reason of her beauty and her activities) to erroneous or hasty interpretations. . . .

> s) A manuscript list of verses which owe their efficacy to their punctuation. (*Labyrinths*, p. 38)

Part of this is an in-joke; he includes the references to Valéry because Valéry's use of an anti-self, M. Teste, provides background for this fiction's attack on selfhood.

One more topic needs to be considered, because it shows that Borges is the quintessential writer of the Literature of Exhaustion. Barth and Nabokov have always been interested in a staple theme of realistic fiction, love, and this has tempered their literary experiments and kept a door open for their return to a more realistic mode. Borges has, however, shown little interest in this theme.

John Updike has speculated on this theme in Borges's writing. He thinks that "physical love, when it appears at all in his work, figures as something remote, like an ancient religion" (p. 235). As for women in Borges's work, Updike writes, "femaleness, far from being identified with, is felt as an estrangement" (p. 235). Updike does find a few references to love in *Dreamtigers*. Borges's poetry provides a few more examples, and "The Aleph" contains a poignant description of an unrequited love for a woman who later dies, although she, Beatriz Viterbo, becomes a pawn for an aesthetic theme. Added together, these examples are still quite meager for a theme that has been so central in literature.

What is the value of all of these things, and of Borges's work in general? Attempts to discredit him can be answered quite well. He writes mainly about literary matters, but Henry James's dictum that we must grant a writer his donnée should justify that attribute. The other serious charge, that he repeats himself, has a good deal of truth to it. But his philosophical reason for being repetitious probably justifies it. In evaluating a body of work as diverse as his, however, general comments have less value than comments on each of the genres he has used.

His poetry seems quite undistinguished. His early contribution to Ultraism may have been important in the history of Spanish literature, but considered from an international viewpoint, Ultraism differs only slightly from the earlier experiments of the Imagists, as Ronald Christ says (p. 4). Borges's poetry intrinsically is competent but hardly of a caliber that would assure him a place in world literature. The change in fashion away from philosophical verse accounts for part of the low evaluation his poetry receives.

His essays are more impressive, because of their grace, originality and wit. The philosophical ones may be too idiosyncratic, because of the ideas they defend and the thinkers they revere, to hold up as philosophy. They do not belong to this category, however, for Borges writes about the ideas and thinkers who have the greatest literary possibilities for him, not those who are the most impressive philosophically. His works in this genre should be considered as occasional essays in the tradition of De Quincey, one of Borges's idols. Thus considered, they come off quite well, well enough to justify some international stature, though not of the greatest magnitude.

The crown of his works is his fiction. Judged in almost any way, it qualifies for the first rank in contemporary literature. The originality of his forms and ideas is indeed impressive. He carefully polishes these works, using a magisterial technique and deftly combining the elements of fiction. And they rank high in a category often ignored by critics: they delight a reader, both because they entertain him and because they provide for him a vicarious experience of a subtle mind at work on fascinating matters.

Besides his work's intrinsic value, it also has heuristic value, since he has inspired many other contemporary writers. He seems to have founded the Literature of Exhaustion, identifying its opponent to be realism and working out its basic themes and techniques. A reader who can thoroughly understand "Tlön, Uqbar, Orbis Tertius" will have a good grasp of this whole movement. Later writers working this same vein merely added a few refinements. The links between him and Beckett, and between him and quite a few American writers should by now be evident. And his affinities with Vladimir Nabokov and John Barth, which are even greater, will become apparent as I consider those writers.

Vladimir Nabokov

Born the same year as Borges, Vladimir Nabokov came later than the Argentinian to the Literature of Exhaustion. This time lag does not necessarily indicate that Borges influenced Nabokov. One always has difficulty substantiating such a claim, especially with a writer as cosmopolitan and erudite as Nabokov, who has lived in Russia, England, Germany, and the United States, immersing himself in the literature of each land and mastering French, Russian, and English. Rather than attributing influence, one should say that these two writers use similar techniques and have similar conceptions about the nature of literature. No misty zeitgeist causes these similarities. Rather, both writers, highly sensitive to the present state of fiction, have the inordinate kind of skill that allows them to take advantage of this situation, and even to do something about it.

Of Nabokov's works, *Lolita* (1955), *Pale Fire* (1962), and *Ada* (1969) belong to the Literature of Exhaustion. He published *Pnin* during this time-span, but it should not be considered part of this literary movement. The three novels appeared appropriately at regular seven year intervals and are his most recent ones besides *Pnin* and the fussy *Transparent Things*. The latter book, although it has few new things in it, deserves an occasional sideways glance. His autobiography, *Speak, Memory* (last version 1966) occasionally illuminates these three novels. Excluding from this study many of his works does not mean that a sharp contrast exists between these late works and his early ones. The seeds that sprouted in his Literature of Exhaustion phase were sown earlier, often even beginning to germinate. For instance, an early novel that recently became available in English, *Mary* (originally written in Russian in 1926), closely resembles vintage Nabokov. Its similarity to later works in style can be explained partly by its recent translation, but its familiar themes and techniques suggest that Nabokov had very early in his career staked out the territory that was to become his.

Many of the books he wrote between *Mary* and *Lolita* resemble his last three novels, *The Gift* (1937) probably being the most notable of them. As he has said, this insufficiently appreciated novel is about Russian literature, so its involution could qualify it to be part of the Literature of Exhaustion. *The Real Life of Sebastian Knight*, his first novel to be written originally in English (1941), has the involuted subject matter of an attempt to understand profoundly an author. In *The Defense* (1930) he creates, mainly through the metaphor of chess, one of his most fully realized imaginary worlds, a world more carefully patterned than the realm usually called real. One can develop quickly a sense of the continuity of Nabokov's canon by reading the last twenty pages of Julian Moynahan's *Vladimir Nabokov*.[1] In this section Moynahan compares *Laughter in the Dark* (1933) with *Lolita*, and *The Gift* with *Pale Fire*. Dealing with all of Nabokov's works, however, or even attempting to trace systematically the roots of his later work, would result in a sprawling discussion and would throw this study out of balance. Therefore, I will restrict myself for the most part to the three novels and the autobiography mentioned earlier as my topics.

The same method that most quickly clarified Borges's work, examining his Chinese boxes, works also with Nabokov. Nabokov constructs Chinese boxes for the same reason that Borges does: to undermine the conventional distinctions between the real and imaginary domains. This similarity of goal and method suggests that these two writers do in fact belong to the same school. In an interview he says, "I think that what I would welcome at the close of a book of mine is a sensation of its world receding in the distance and stopping somewhere there suspended afar like a picture in a picture: *The Artist's Studio* by Van Bock."[2] He, of course, is Van

Bock and the painting is imaginary, a metaphor for his idea of perfect art. In *Transparent Things* the boundary between his fictional world and the books created by a novelist who is a character in the novel keep shifting. Confused about what is real, a reader tends to admit that Nabokov himself controls reality. In *Lolita* and *Ada* he makes an effort to paint such a picture within a picture by claiming that imaginary editors have worked over the manuscripts. John Ray, Jr., the alleged editor of *Lolita*, even writes a brief foreword that serves as a frame tale. The imaginary editor of *Ada*, Ronald Oranger, effaces himself more completely. These Chinese boxes, however, are simple compared to Borges's.

Nabokov uses Chinese boxes most subtly in *Pale Fire*, and in that book he makes them crucial to the meaning. In this novel, Nabokov is the outermost layer, followed by *Pale Fire*, which, like "Tlön, Uqbar, Orbis Tertius" and for the same reasons, contains the dividing line between the real and the imaginary. Botkin, the fairly well hidden teller of the tale, is the third layer, and the pseudonym he uses, Kinbote, is the fourth layer. Next come the commentary and the index, which tell the story of Zembla and its king. Patricia Merivale has clarified the relation between this layer and the one inside it by correctly identifying an allusion that supplies an important clue.[3] Most critics have followed one of Nabokov's false trails, deducing from the many references to Pope in *Pale Fire* that the Zembla mentioned in *Essay on Man* is the relevant one. That reference, however, either does not apply or, if a relation is forced, the subject matter of the quotation from Pope puts *Pale Fire* in a moral light, in which it will not be able to live for long. In Swift's *Battle of the Books*, however, "a malignant Deity, call'd *Criticism*" lives on a mountain in Nova Zembla. This malignant deity and its priest, Kinbote, obfuscate the next layer, John Shade's poem "Pale Fire." The last layer is Shade, who belongs inside his poem rather than outside it because he has written an autobiographical work that reveals, and in a sense controls, him.

Except for the absence of infinite possibilities, Nabokov's boxes appear similar to Borges's. A reader of the criticism of *Pale Fire*, however, should realize, first, that Nabokov's method for disrupting the common notions about reality differs from Borges's method, and second, that at least in regard to some critics, Nabokov's method has worked. Very cleverly, he makes the five-part series of imagined layers reversible. The authors of two of the full-length studies of his work disagree on the correct order of these layers. Andrew Field believes that Shade created Kinbote, wrote the commentary as well as the poem and therefore should be called the "primary author."[4] Page Stegner claims exactly the opposite: "It is even possible, perhaps probable, that Gradus and Shade are as much figments of Kinbote's imagination as Charles the Beloved and the far-distant land of Zembla. Although it is difficult, if this is true, to explain where the poem came from, it is conceivable that Kinbote could have written it himself."[5] In other words, Stegner's theory fits the order of the boxes that I gave, but Field's requires placing Shade's layer, because he considers it to be the most real, next to the *Pale Fire* layer and reversing the order I listed.

One must resist the temptation to arbitrate between Field and Stegner or to decide who is correct. Rather, one should conclude that they both have swallowed Nabokov's bait. That is, they disagree about where "reality" resides in a work of the imagination. Actually, the author and his book (the latter in one sense only) are real; any layer inside them—actually *in* the novel—is imaginary, and none of these inside layers has more reality than any other. Field and Stegner inadvertently lend credence to Nabokov's contention that the imaginary can be more "real" than "reality" and, its corollary, that the "real" is in truth imaginary. Next he claims that the imagination is the supreme, if not the only, reality. Out of these ideas arise the central paradoxes of the Literature of Exhaustion: this kind of literature creates, by using the premise that the imaginary realm of fiction is exhausted, works of fiction that assert the primacy of the imagination and add to the total number of fictional works.

Besides the Chinese box technique, a critic can use another way to visualize the levels of reality in *Pale Fire*. It can be derived from

Nabokov's frequent references, especially in *Ada*, to forkings. This scheme emphasizes the disjunction in *Pale Fire* between the poem and the critical apparatus. It does not conflict with the previous arrangement, but is a more esoteric variant. The bifurcation begins after the *Pale Fire* level, and it can be represented by a two-dimensional drawing of divergent paths. One path leads from Botkin to Kinbote to the commentary and index. The commentary doubles back on Kinbote rather than connecting with the poem, because in it he tells his own story or cries out in alarm over a psychological trauma. It certainly does not explicate the poem accurately. The other path begins with Shade and ends with the poem. Shade attempts to make the poem self-enclosed, to perpetrate (in the words of Stegner's title) an escape into aesthetics. But he fails and his work, like Kinbote's, turns back on its creator. This alternate schematization, by insisting that poem and criticism do not meet, brings to mind a theory of Susan Sontag's that, although it explains only a few of the phenomena that comprise the Literature of Exhaustion, does not seem discordant with my understanding of this kind of literature. She claims that writers have deliberately created much of the opacity of contemporary literature as their reaction to the flood of criticism that has swept over their work. She fully delineates her argument and gives illustrative examples in her provocative *Against Interpretation*.

Nabokov uses the Literature of Exhaustion's companion image to the Chinese boxes, the infinite regress, as much as Borges does, and they both cite the instance of Achilles and the Tortoise, though Nabokov reverses chaser and chased. In *Ada* appears the theory that "the Tortoise of the Past will never overtake the Achilles of the future, no matter how we parse distances on our cloudy blackboards."[6] The other of Zeno's two famous paradoxes looms larger than this one in Nabokov's work. He uses this paradox—the arrowhead moving toward a target in the same unsuccessful way that Achilles moves toward the tortoise—to make the same point that he makes with the paradox of the tortoise. His most subtle application of the principle on which these paradoxes are built can be found in the structure of *Ada*. As this book progresses, the action seems to be speeded up; late in the book he describes fewer events in, say each one-year time span, and those he does describe have much less lavish detail than do the earlier events. This effect of memory failing to catch up in its recreation of the past resembles the sensation Achilles must have felt, as it were, when he realized that he was closing the gap but never closing it altogether. Nabokov describes the earlier events in a more leisurely way since they have been caressed for a longer time by memory than the later events have been. Worked over less thoroughly by memory, the later events seem more disembodied and also seem gradually to recede and to hang suspended, from memory, like the painting Nabokov spoke about in the *Contemporary Literature* interview. But unlike the target and the tortoise, the events in *Ada* never completely escape their pursuer to become purely aesthetic artifacts. The memory that in the first place shaped them into art always maintains some connection with them, and so does the everyday world.

Nabokov's opinion about the reality of that everyday world to a large extent determines the kind of literature that he writes. He shares with Borges one of his main premises, that realism is misguided, though he does not hold to this premise quite as rigorously as the other writer. His bluntest statement about the status of reality appears in his *Paris Review* interview, when he says simply that "everyday reality" does not exist.[7] The most important word in this phrase of course is "everyday," for he does not subscribe to nihilism; he merely believes that other kinds of reality have more claim to men's allegiance. Sometimes he uses more clever and more indirect methods to convince readers of this. Readers of *Pale Fire* who can step back and see what kind of responses they have been limited to by the book can understand that they have been tricked into taking their eyes off the everyday world. A reader of *Pale Fire* must choose from among three entities that claim to be real. One is the poem, away from which Kinbote, the second entity, turns almost completely. Once a reader sees the discrepancy between the poem and Kinbote's criticism, he seeks a third entity to serve as a touchstone, and he can find one in the fictive realm that the novel creates. However, this novel has two settings: Zembla and New Wye, and two different actions. This complicated interaction among rival realities demands the reader's attention, so he turns his back on the everyday world from which he emerged to read the novel. At least while he reads *Pale Fire*, if he does not resist the author's pressure, he sets aside everyday reality, and perhaps this will become habit forming.

This game of illusions in *Pale Fire* also includes an epistemological puzzle. An examination of the sources of information in this novel reveals that, among many other things, it considers metaphorically the types of fiction. A reader can see this most easily if he sets aside the minor characters and then analyzes how he knows about Shade and Kinbote (for convenience, I will refer to this pseudonym and forget the almost invisible character who assumes it, Botkin). Once a reader understands the ground rules of the book, he starts applying the label "true" to the data he gets about Shade from his poem. It would be carrying skepticism too far to doubt the facts presented in a seemingly straight-forward autobiographical poem.

With this data as a basis, the next step is to divide into "true" and "false" the information about Shade that comes from the commentary. For example, the things one learns about his methods of writing seem true, because Kinbote has no reason to deceive a reader about them and because they do not contradict anything in the poem. On the other hand, one should doubt Kinbote's assessment of Shade's affection for him, because Kinbote has a stake in this and his self-flattering assessment does not accord with the scarcity of references to Kinbote in the poem. Shade makes practically no references to Kinbote in the poem, so nearly all the knowledge about the relation between them, perhaps all of it, comes from the commentary. A reader's reaction to this knowledge differs very much from his reaction to the knowledge about Shade. For this knowledge the proper labels are to be "hidden" and "manifest," because the reader tries to discern Kinbote's identity by reading between the lines of his eccentric—less charitably, mad—statements. A reader who has realized that Kinbote has tricked him will not accept anything he says at face value but rather will probe deeper for hidden meanings. In other words, one naturally treats the information about Shade as if it came from a realistic novel (one that purports to tell the truth) and the information about Kinbote as if it came from a nonrealistic novel (one that creates patterns, some more manifest than others). To add an evaluation, the facts of Shade's life are considerably less interesting than the discoveries one makes trying to figure out Kinbote, which strengthens Nabokov's case against the realistic novel.

Nabokov has other allies besides Borges to help him argue his case against realism, which he considers to have exhausted its meager possibilities. Stegner convincingly establishes for him a tradition: impressionism. He says: "Impressionism is a statement of the subjectivity of reality and the variety of individual responses to collective experience. . . . Reality, insofar as it is definable, is primarily the images and impressions in the mind" (p. 45). Despite its usefulness, this statement needs slight modification. One must use greater care in ascribing general ideas like these to Nabokov than in ascribing them to other writers. Also, Stegner wrote his book before *Ada,* in which Nabokov makes somewhat of a rapprochement with everyday reality. Stegner develops his idea in a full chapter and also alludes to other critics who have dealt with this kind of literature, and, with these two minor caveats, his discussion sheds a good deal of light on Nabokov.

Among Nabokov's books, *Pale Fire* makes the most persuasive case that genuine reality must be found in unexpected places and can be discovered only by unusual means. In the *TriQuarterly* Nabokov issue Nina Berberova describes this novel with the kind of insight that at first seems startling and then seems perfectly clear and obvious. She points out a significant reversal: this novel's symbolic level lies on its surface and its realistic level lies hidden.[8] This phenomenon, like many in the Literature of Exhaustion, encourages readers to reconsider their ideas about the nature of reality. A reader will be even more likely to reconsider his ideas if he can have another startlingly obvious insight. That is, if he can follow Nabokov's clues and penetrate Kinbote's illusions, he will discover that Zembla does not exist except as a figment of the imagination. But should this not be completely obvious? After all, Zembla is not only a country in a novel, but it is also an imaginary country even according to the norms of that novel.

At this point a reader must resist the temptation to call Nabokov a solipsist. He does not consider any subjective conception of reality to be valid merely because it is subjective. But Nabokov makes clear the madness of Humbert Humbert and, especially, of Kinbote. Stegner claims that the former cannot distinguish the reality of the imagination from the reality of everyday life (p. 115). He errs slightly, because if Lolita represents everyday reality and Humbert's conception of her represents the reality of the imagination, Humbert seems capable of distinguishing between the two. He frequently describes Lolita as merely a vulgar young girl. His mental error is trying to transform this reality into something else. Setting aside conventional morality and trying to see his actions in the context of the fictional world that Nabokov creates, one can see that Humbert makes a mistake but not a heinous one. He does try to connect imagination with reality, a process that his creator sometimes spurns because it spoils the purity of the imagination. He could, however, have committed a more serious sin: trying to make the imagination conform to reality, the sin of the realistic novelists.

Again according to the rules of Nabokov's world, Kinbote's error is genuine but only venial. Like Humbert, he tries to connect his imaginative construct with something else, but for this other thing he chooses another imaginative construct, Shade's poem. His delusion remains innocent, even interesting, as long as it remains self-enclosed, but then he mistakenly claims that he can explicate "Pale Fire." Kinbote's Zembla is nearly as fanciful as the imaginary realms in Ada, but in the latter work Nabokov goes out of his way to see that as few as possible of the points he makes about Terra and

Anti-Terra seem like satiric barbs hurled against targets in reality. In short, he argues in *Lolita* and *Pale Fire* that the imagination is superior to everyday reality but that people must not try to connect imaginative creations with that other reality or with anyone else's imaginative creation.

In *Ada* Nabokov less vigorously opposes everyday reality than he does in his two previous books. At least, he hesitates to attack the part of reality that contains nature. His more mellow attitude includes respect for another way of knowing besides literature: science. This new position should hardly seem surprising in light of his fascination, since childhood, with nature. He is a lepidopterist of professional competence and the author of a number of scientific articles. Before his most recent novel, however, he had used his scientific knowledge mainly as a source of metaphors, but in *Ada* the title character is a scientist. Also, she and her lover/brother, Van, a philosopher and writer, represent, for one thing, the two sides of their creator's personality. The incest theme in this novel functions partly to show that scientific and literary interests can exist harmoniously in the same person. It follows from this compatibility that the imagination can also connect with reality, because "reality and natural science are synonymous in the terms of this, and only this, dream" (p. 67). The dream is the imaginative world of *Ada*.

Nabokov still does not believe that everyday reality and science, and the common domain of both—nature—can replace the imagination as the dominant reality. A writer, however, can make metaphors from them. Ada, because of her scientific training, has a higher opinion than Van of the world of nature, but Nabokov points out her mistake. Early in the novel she says: "But *this* . . . is certain, this is reality, this is pure fact—this forest, this moss, your hand, the ladybird on my leg, this cannot be taken away, can it? (it will, it was)" (p. 123). And later in the book Ada herself loses much of her fascination with science. Science commits sins of omission, not commission; within its limits science and its object of study, nature, are wondrous. In this novel Nabokov does not maintain his earlier interest in nature as a freak show, a conception that also denigrates science. Mary McCarthy has documented the existence of this attitude in *Pale Fire* by making an impressively long list of freaks and shams in it, like "the arrowy tracks of the pheasant, the red heraldic barrings of the Vanessa butterfly, snow crystals."[9] Rather, in *Ada* Nabokov draws exquisite, nearly paradisiacal nature scenes, and he uses the full splendor of his prose style to describe a nature that is anything but hostile to man's imagination.

Even in *Ada*, however, nature by itself cannot nourish man. Its beauty serves only as material for the imagination to turn into art. Clearly, Nabokov himself has done this, both in his set-piece descriptions of nature and in the natural metaphors and images that he sprinkles so thickly throughout the novel. If somehow the reader misses this transformation of nature, Nabokov provides a hint—typically, in a passage that at first glance confuses or slips past the reader. This passage describes the scrabble game in which Ada makes a phenomenal score by using the Russian word for peaty. To underline this hint a negotiation soon begins for the sale of peat bogs. The meaning of peat in the novel becomes evident if one realizes that it is a natural substance being transformed.

Another branch of realistic writing, autobiography, plays a complicated role in Nabokov's work. *Speak, Memory* provides much data about his life and makes it possible to determine how he uses autobiographical information in his fiction. The most obvious use has been to supply biographical facts and opinions to his fictional characters. In *Pale Fire* he parcels these out to both Kinbote and Shade. Like Nabokov, Shade writes on index cards and once nearly burned a draft of one of his works (in Nabokov's case, *Lolita*). One section of Shade's "Pale Fire" also attacks some things that Nabokov himself has inveighed against in interviews:

> I loathe such things as jazz;
> The white-hosed moron torturing a black
> Bull, rayed with red; abstractist bric-a-brac;
> Primitivist folk-masks; progressive schools;

Music in supermarkets; swimming pools;
Brutes, bores, class-conscious Philistines, Freud, Marx,
Fake thinkers, puffed-up poets, frauds and sharks.

(p. 47)

About the only discrepancy between Shade's list and Nabokov's
bête noires appears in the picture that the *TriQuarterly* printed of
Nabokov, in shorts and cap, writing beside the Montreux Palace
Hotel's swimming pool. Kinbote, like many Nabokov characters,
shares with his creator the special pangs of the exile, and unique
among these characters but like Nabokov, he has written a detailed,
personalized set of notes to a poem. The appropriate analogue of
Kinbote's edition is of course Nabokov's edition of *Eugene Onegin*, which he wrote about the same time that he wrote *Pale Fire*.
In *Pale Fire* Nabokov describes this borrowing of details, the most
common use of autobiographical data in composing and criticizing
literature: *"Man's life as a commentary to abstruse | Unfinished
poem"* (p. 48).

But this banal and realistic use makes Nabokov skeptical. He
expresses this doubt in the opening of "Pale Fire" after the haunting, often quoted first two lines:

I was the smudge of ashen fluff—and I
Lived on, flew on, in the reflected sky.
And from the inside, too, I'd duplicate
Myself, my lamp, an apple on a plate:

(p. 23)

The first two of these lines describe Shade's hope for some kind of
immortality, either in an afterlife or in eternally enduring art. His
hopes for the latter will probably be dashed by his decision to write
autobiographical poetry. His mistake appears in the last two lines
of this quotation: Nabokov shows that when Shade looks at possible
subject matter he sees only himself. Literally, this happens because
of the mirror effect of the window through which he looks. Figura-
tively, it happens because of his false conception of art. The quotation from *Timon of Athens* (act 4, scene 3, lines 439ff) that provides
the novel's title shows why autobiography is negative:

> The sun's a thief, and with his great attraction
> Robs the vast sea; the moon's an arrant thief,
> And her pale fire she snatches from the sun:

Most critics claim that this allusion relates to Kinbote's robbery of Shade's poem, but the things that Kinbote purports to take from "Pale Fire" really do not exist. Most likely, they refer to Shade's robbery, in his poetry, of his own life. He does take things that exist, and he uses this allusion.

Shade's use of his own life as subject matter is wrong because this use duplicates something that already exists, rather than creating infinite possibilities. This same attitude toward thievery from one's life appears in, of all places, *Speak, Memory*, where Nabokov says that real things from his life, after he puts them into his books, lose all contact with his life, passing completely from one distinct realm to another. That is, autobiographical material must, in a sense, become nonautobiographical when a writer uses it in fiction. These ideas cast a new light on *Pale Fire*. Readers have recognized from the beginning its ironic comment, by means of Kinbote, on Nabokov's edition of *Eugene Onegin*. If I have correctly delineated the autobiographical theme in this novel, it also comments ironically, by means of Shade, on *Speak, Memory* in particular and, in general, on Nabokov's use of autobiography in his fiction. If so, he does not necessarily contradict himself or recant his earlier works; he merely uses an attack on autobiography as an interesting hypothesis to create more literature. His premise that autobiography should not intrude into fiction follows from the Literature of Exhaustion's main theorem.

These ways of looking at the autobiographical elements in Nabokov's work assume that his life and personality are static and completely formed, but one can also consider these things to be in flux. In his *Annotated Lolita* Alfred Appel maintains that Nabokov's "art records a constant process of becoming—the evolution of the artist's self through artistic creation."[10] That is, it may be wrong to separate the writer as man from the writer as writer, for as he uses the material from the first of these parts of his personality he builds up the other part. Appel's idea also implies that one should look at life itself as artistic, and adopting this viewpoint will help one understand Nabokov's use of autobiography.

In *Speak, Memory* Nabokov claims that although life may exist independently of art it can only be understood by means of art. In his first chapter he states this basic premise of this distinctive autobiography: "Neither in environment nor in heredity can I find the exact instrument that fashioned me, the anonymous roller that pressed upon my life a certain intricate watermark whose unique design becomes visible when the lamp of art is made to shine through life's foolscap" (p. 18). If this is true, the autobiographer must use the techniques of the novelist, and on the next page Nabokov states this corollary: "the following of such thematic designs through one's life should be, I think, the true purpose of autobiography." And he does this in his autobiography, organizing it thematically, with chronology as only a subsidiary organizing principle. His life becomes comprehensible not through a linear tracing of the main events in it in the order in which they happened but through the emergence of thread after thread of the figure in the carpet. That is, he creates thematic pattern after thematic pattern.

This last idea shows that his use of autobiographical material only apparently contradicts his complaint about using it. Material is material; in the broadest sense one must write out of his experience, if not directly, then by combining bits of knowledge or experience. The real issue is the way the artist uses this material. The artist must not assume that he can use it unchanged or, more generally, that the world has an order which need only be perceived and used as the order of art. Instead he must subject this chaotic material to the only genuine ordering force in the world, art. Therefore, art has dominion over everyday reality, including its autobiographical sector.

Nabokov's relation to the other kinds of subject matter used by the realistic writer—for example, sociology, politics, history and psychology—is less complicated than his relation to autobiography.

His remark in *Speak, Memory* about patterns in autobiography succinctly clarifies his attitude toward them. According to *Nabokov: The Man and His Work* he said, "I have always maintained . . . that the nationality of a worthwhile writer is of secondary importance. . . . The writer's art is his real passport. His identity should be immediately recognized by a special pattern or unique coloration" (p. 19). Inevitably, however, some social description and commentary appear in his recent works. He allows more of it in earlier works like *Bend Sinister* and *Invitation to a Beheading*, but even in those works he makes only very general social comments. He makes his most notable sociological comments in his late novels by describing America in *Lolita*, but anyone who reads this novel as a rebuttal of the American Automobile Association's travel guides misses the mark by as much as one can. Nabokov transmutes the tawdry setting, like the nymphetomania, into art, just as Humbert's imagination transmutes Lolita into a glorious creature. Critics who point out the tawdriness but not the transmutation make a damaging comment on themselves.

Nabokov makes so many quotable satiric comments on a branch of psychology, Freudianism, that all of his readers know his attitude toward it. They abound in his books and in interviews; in fact, Alfred Appel once deliberately brought up this old subject to see if Nabokov had stored up still another *mot*. He had. He complains for several reasons: that Freudianism oversimplifies and obfuscates with jargon, and, most important, that it subordinates artistic creation to psychological processes. He also makes sure that Freudianism and other schools of psychology do not satisfactorily explain his characters. For example, he plants hints that Freudians will pick up and then leads those who fall for them down a false trail. He does this when he presents the facts of Humbert's early life. However, Nabokov's interest in the motives of his characters differentiates him from Borges. He traces these motives by his own special methods, and before very long these motives lead to a clarification not so much of the character but of a theme, usually an aesthetic theme. For example, in his final appearance in *Lolita*,

Quilty's actions derive mainly from Nabokov's desire to parody the convention of the double. By using human personality in this way he makes once again the point that art triumphs over reality.

Just as Nabokov and Borges shun the same kinds of literature, they also produce the same kinds. Nabokov's work, too, continually cries out that it is art or artifice. In his recent work he gradually develops from creating quite conventional types of artifice in *Lolita* and *Pale Fire* to creating more original and subtle types in *Ada*. All three novels, however, clearly belong to the Literature of Exhaustion. *Lolita* contains notes purportedly written by proofreaders and included by mistake, and the hand of the master always pokes through holes in his puppets' costumes. He continually suggests that another person is using the narrator as a ventriloquist's dummy; for example, he reveals information that Humbert cannot know He also has Quilty, too, supply information that this character has no plausible way of knowing. The peculiar form of *Pale Fire*—poem and critical commentary—calls attention to this novel's artificiality, too.

He does not abandon this technique in *Ada*. Ada's marginal notes and interpolated passages of narrative, editor's notes and even study questions and a blurb at the very end of the novel perform the same function that the artificial devices in the other books do. Nabokov also underscores the fact that *Ada* is a novel by frequently referring to other novels and commenting on narrative technique. At one point he breaks the story-line and inserts a description of a landau, "from which emerged . . . the Erminin twins, their young pregnant aunt (narrationally a great burden), and a governess, white-haired Mme Forestier, the school friend of Mathilde in a forthcoming story" (p. 68). Nabokov even helpfully points out lines of analysis for inattentive readers: "when lightning struck two days later (an old image that is meant to intimate a flash-back to an old barn)" (p. 219).

He uses this artifice more originally when he insists that parts of *Ada* are paintings. This technique has been used before—Henry James does something similar late in *The Ambassadors* to indicate that Strether has developed a painterly sensibility—but Nabokov uses it uniquely. In his most impressive example he describes a frolic by Van, Ada, and Lucette. It begins "thus seen from above, as if reflected in the ciel mirror that Eric had naively thought up in his Cyprian dreams" (p. 319). Given the mannered, elongated picture that follows, the Cyprian dream probably represents El Greco's Cretan dream. He frames this painting at the other end by paradoxically announcing: "unsigned and unframed" (p. 320).

The section in between the two frames describes some fascinating metamorphoses. In its first stage he uses the familiar novelistic device of the love triangle. Then, however, he actuates this dead metaphor by placing the three people in the triangle in bed together; that is, he turns a metaphor into the second stage, a literal arrangement in space. Then by means of a peculiar kind of description this space reaches the third stage, geographical space; for instance, "the top sheet and quilt are tumbled at the footboardless south of the island where the newly landed eye starts on its northern trip" (p. 319). Since this concept of space comes in a string of artificial constructs, the reader has trouble resisting the conclusion that geography, and indeed all kinds of science, are artificial constructs like any other and not the construct by which one should measure the others. This geographical description then gives way to the fourth stage, a painterly description; he turns geography metaphorically into painting. The painting creates artistic, rather than scientific, space. It also changes into the fifth stage, fiction, because, after all, this is a passage in a novel. These transformations and the meanings of each phase add "texture" to space as throughout the novel Nabokov adds texture to time. The multitude of references to painters in the novel reinforces this transformation into painting. He contrasts painting with photography, which Kim practices maliciously to blackmail Ada and Van. Morally in error, Kim's photographs realistically depict nontextured space and are also therefore inferior to painting. Nabokov would probably also argue that they are analogous to realistic novels, because they lack texture, and that his own fiction—the works I am calling the Literature of Exhaustion—are textured like paintings. Maybe Pater's famous statement needs modification: all art aspires to the condition of painting.

Carl Proffer saw the painterly side of Nabokov's sensibility even before it reached its fullest expression in *Ada*. In *Keys to Lolita* he mentions many of the passages in *Lolita* that describe sun and shade.[11] Later he discusses the author's "obsession with colors" and a possible cause of it, his "colored hearing" (Nabokov believes that each linguistic sound has a corresponding color) (p. 110). The former insight leads further than the latter, which too simply psychologizes away an unusual phenomenon. A convincing reason for the abundance of color in Nabokov's work appears in *Speak, Memory*, but it is a philosophical, not a psychological, reason. He conceives of the time spans before consciousness is formed and after death as darknesses. Then he says, "I see the awakening of consciousness as a series of spaced flashes, with the intervals between them gradually diminishing until bright blocks of perception are formed, affording memory a slippery hold" (p. 14). As these flashes of light become colored they become more textured. The painting motif in *Ada*, then, captures more territory for consciousness, particularly for the consciousness of the artist. Then an artist adds texture to his material; in other words, he adds vitality and meaning to it. And Nabokov also makes it clear that in the process the artist creates artifice.

Again like Borges, Nabokov uses an enormous number of allusions, but unlike Borges, he sometimes misleads with his allusions. Often he plants them in order to lead down wrong paths critics who think they can match learning with him. One must be particularly wary of the allusions in *Lolita*, which can cause many frustrated expectations. Most of the references to Poe's works and to Merimeé's *Carmen* create false scents, the latter because they indicate that Humbert will kill Lolita. Nabokov also refers to his own work much more often than Borges does, but a reader can easily spot these references. The allusions in *Lolita* have been doggedly tracked down, especially by Carl Proffer, in *Keys to Lolita*, and Alfred Appel, in *The Annotated Lolita*. Some good work has also been done on this aspect of *Pale Fire* and *Ada*, but a bit more is needed.

Mary McCarthy's article in *Encounter* identifies many of the allusions in *Pale Fire* but some of her purported finds seem bogus. Nabokov correctly comments that "she added quite a bit of her own angelica to the pale fire of Kinbote's plum pudding."[12] Read with some skepticism, though, her article provides a valuable beginning. She and other critics have found most of the allusions from eighteenth century British literature. Patricia Merivale's point in *Nabokov: The Man and His Work* about the Zembla in *Battle of the Books* explains one allusion to eighteenth century literature, and John O. Lyons adds more of the needed information about the role of Pope and Swift in this novel (p. 214; p. 159). Other bits and pieces about these two writers appear in McCarthy's article, Appel's edition and elsewhere. Taken together, these allusions indicate that Kinbote inadvertently plays Swift to Shade's Pope, which demonstrates Kinbote's madness, not because Swift's organic malady finally got the better of him but because with his role-playing Kinbote tries to bend the real world to fit the world of literature. Andrew Field finds, but misuses, some more eighteenth century material. He has discovered that the epigraph of *Pale Fire* and a description of Boswell's aborted plans to get Johnson to write about the Boswells appear on the same page of *The Life of Johnson*. With tortuous logic Field tries to show from this juxtaposition that Shade imagined Kinbote. Rather, this phenomenon shows that Kinbote wants to be Shade's Boswell, to produce a biography of the great man, and he hopes, like Boswell, that his subject will reciprocate. To support this interpretation, people think that Shade looks like Johnson (p. 188). More to the point, Nabokov once drops a hint about this matter, having Kinbote first refer to a footnote from *The Life of Johnson*, and then write a Boswellian dialogue: "talking of the vulgarity of a certain burly acquaintance of ours: 'The man is as corny as a cook-out chef apron.' Kinbote (laughing): 'Wonderful!' " and so on in the same vein (p. 112). Like the Pope and Swift allusions, these allusions demonstrate that literature can determine life, which in turn leads to the Literature of Exhaustion's belief in the primacy of the imagination.

No one seems to have carried through with the *Timon of Athens* reference after someone found the source of *Pale Fire's* title in Shakespeare's play. This allusion needs to be further clarified because in a sense *Pale Fire* is Nabokov's version of that play. Shade, in his charitable actions, like his tolerance of Kinbote, resembles Timon before his disasters and resulting misanthropy. Kinbote, wanting Shade to himself, tries to believe that the poet is like the reclusive Timon of later years. If Shade resembles Timon, Kinbote resembles the homosexual Alcibiades, who, as Plutarch reports in his life of Antony, was banished from Athens and subsequently met Timon. Kinbote again has tried to make life and literature fit each other. Some of the references to Russian literature also need explanation. Shade is like Nabokov's revered Pushkin because of his autobiographical poetry and his death by gunshot. *Pale Fire* also has a reference to Lermontov's *Hero of Our Time*, which Nabokov has translated and which, like *Pale Fire*, has a story within a story.

Ada, despite its recent publication, has been quite thoroughly searched for allusions. John Updike, Robert Alter, and Alfred Appel have found and explained the references to Chateaubriand, Tolstoy, Marvell's "The Garden," and some less important sources, Carl Proffer has identified many allusions to Russian literature, and other critics have also made useful contributions.[13] To these sources I would add *Through the Looking Glass*, which Nabokov also translated and which has influenced him throughout his career. Carroll's Alice has a sister named Ada and both books have the theme of the imaginary mirror world. Also, no one seems to have mentioned the poem that, along with "The Garden," is Ada and Van's favorite, Rimbaud's "Mémoire." The memory theme and the yearning for an idyllic lost childhood dominate this poem. As "The Garden" creates a timeless present, "Mémoire" creates a timeless past. The title of Van's favorite novel, *The Slat Sign*, also looks like a clue to an allusion, perhaps in anagrammatic form. Not being able to turn it into an anagram or a Russian pun, I believe that it should be taken to mean just what it says, a slat sign, the most common kind being armed services recruiting signs. These signs have slats extended from them at right angles so that a person passing in front of them will see a sign on one side of the slats, another on the flat surface and a third on the other side of the slats. The effect is very like reading and analyzing a Nabokov novel.

Nabokov does not merely play games with all these allusions. True, because of them and other features, reading him is sometimes exasperating. Stegner aptly describes this feeling: "like playing a long tiresome game of Scrabble and losing" (p. 131). He needs these allusions, however, to demonstrate that authors make literature, above all, from other literature, not from life. This belief is, by itself, one of the precursors of the Literature of Exhaustion and, combined with other attitudes, part of that kind of literature.

Sometimes he makes his work not only from, but also about, literature. As Appel says, after granting the Russian émigrée critic Khodasevich the honor of being the first to propose it, this notion about Nabokov has become a commonplace. This aspect of his work appears in the play within *Lolita*, which recapitulates that novel. The characters in it include "a Young Poet, and he insisted, much to Diana's annoyance, that she and the entertainment provided (dancing nymphs, and elves, and monsters) were his, the Poet's, invention" (p. 184). Just as these things exist in the poet's imagination, so do Lolita's magic qualities exist only in Humbert's imagination. And of course all these things and many more exist in Nabokov's imagination. A poet's reality can be distinct from, rather than an imitation of, everyday reality. In one of his lucid moments Kinbote in *Pale Fire* makes a claim that his creator would accept: " 'reality' is neither the subject nor the object of true art which creates its own special reality having nothing to do with the average 'reality' perceived by the communal eye" (p. 94). Ecstasy unknown to the artistically untalented, not aesthetic schizophrenia, produces this private reality. In "On a Book Entitled *Lolita*" Nabokov asserts that this magical condition exists: "a work of fiction exists only insofar as it affords me what I shall bluntly call aesthetic bliss, that is a sense of being somehow, somewhere, connected with other states of being where art (curiosity, tenderness, kindness, ecstasy) is the norm" (*Lolita*, p. 286). In this statement he rebukes readers who demand, or believe that they will always find, a moral in literature, and he argues convincingly that one should not bother about morality when he can have bliss.

In literature this bliss usually takes the form of wonder at the adroit use of man's greatest invention, language, and this wonder is most intense when the wonderer himself is the linguistic master. This awakening to language, one of the characteristic episodes in *Künstlerromanen*, happens to Van in *Ada*. After his initial fervid sexual encounter with Ada, "for the first time in their love story, the blessing, the genius of lyrical speech descended upon the rough lad" (p. 98). Many times Nabokov has connected art with ardor as he does here. John Shade's wife Sybil, though kept out of the commentary as much as possible by the jealous Kinbote, seems to be a muse-figure, defending her favorite's creative powers from the malevolent critic. Her name suits a muse. Véra Nabokov, to whom Nabokov dedicates most of his books, plays the same role in real life. The splendor of language is not the paltry thing implied by Humbert when he cries out, in his agony over losing the elusive Lolita, that he has only words to play with (p. 32). Humbert should know better, since his awakening to words comes on the first page of the novel, when he breaks speech into sheer sounds and marvels at the result.

Like Borges, Nabokov manages to be literary without being mythic. In fact, he manages better than Borges, so well that critics have almost completely avoided using myth criticism on his work. Mary McCarthy, nearly the only exception, makes a discreet mythic analysis as she tries to prove only that Gradus may be modelled on Mercury (p. 81). She cites the statue of that god in the passageway that leads from the palace to the theater, an image that more likely refers to Mercury's role as the conductor of souls to the underworld. The journey down to escape—from, for one thing, Disa, King

Charles's wife, whose name sounds like a feminine form of Dis, an underworld god—is like a descent into Hell in order to rise again into Paradise, as Dante did. The only other important mythic element in Nabokov's work is also obvious, the comparisons of Ardis Hall and its environs in *Ada* to Eden.

Nabokov prefers to play games rather than make myths. His work, besides its allusions, contains many puns—sometimes multilingual—anagrams and other puzzles. Most of these produce one of two fleeting effects, depending on whether or not the reader understands them: a feeling of satisfaction and perhaps a chuckle or an annoyed grunt. Many of his puns make fun of Freud: Lajoyeux, Froid, Signy-Mondieu-Mondieu. Once in a while Nabokov plays for higher stakes, as he does when he composes an anagram in *Ada*. The three main characters form three anagrams from "insect": "scient," "incest" and "nicest." It would be possible to organize around these four words a fairly perceptive analysis of this novel, since they introduce the love, nature, and philosophy themes, evaluate them and hint at the tone of the book.

Characteristically, Nabokov plays these games to discredit realism. For one thing, they distract the reader from character conflicts, social background and other elements that would lead him to a realistic interpretation of this novel. To put it another way, Nabokov's novels are to realistic novels as solving chess problems is to playing chess. In *Speak, Memory* Nabokov compares writing novels to composing chess problems, for in both the battle is not between the pieces on the board but between the person who placed them in position and the solver, who tries to see the pattern (p. 214). For another thing, these games provide the reader with a glimpse of a plane of existence more fascinatingly intricate than the mundane world. In the world of magic, the most appropriate metaphor for this plane, exotic, law-defying things happen and the magician has total control. Kinbote compares Shade to a conjurer, "perceiving and transforming the world, taking it in and taking it apart, recombining its elements in the very process of storing them up so as to produce at some unspecified date an organic miracle, a fusion of image and music, a line of verse" (p. 18). Nabokov makes the same comparison between art and magic in *Speak, Memory*, and compares nature to both (p. 92).

Nabokov manipulates the conventions of various genres with as much dexterity as Borges. Van Veen claims that " 'old storytelling devices . . . may be parodied only by very great and inhuman artists" (p. 189). If so, Nabokov is very great and inhuman. Depending on his intent, he parodies or imitates a great number of genres: in *Lolita*, the case study, the novel of the double, detective stories and pornography; in *Pale Fire*, the critical edition; and in *Ada*, letters, essays and the drama. He uses other genres most impressively in *Pale Fire*, because his use is probably original and because he keeps it up for the entire book. In it, mere parody soon gives way to creative imitation, and he invents a new hybrid form for future novelists.

He creates these imitations and parodies again to dispute realism. There are two ways to look at his strategy: from the reader's point of view and from the technical point of view. As to the former, in the *TriQuarterly* Nabokov issue Appel says that in *Ada* Nabokov parodies the conceptions of the reader, setting him free to experience the work aesthetically. As to the latter, Stegner makes the shrewd point that "when a writer adopts a convention, he takes along with it certain implicit perceptions; in short, he accepts with stock methods a stock view of reality" (p. 35). He concludes that Nabokov, by parodying conventions, can impose his own view of reality on his subject and can suggest "that man is capable of *manipulating* reality through art" (p. 35).

Nabokov performs a still more prodigious feat with genre in *Ada*. Van Veen announces that he aims to write an investigation of time and to form out of its illustrative metaphors a love story, and Nabokov himself does exactly this. The simplest example of a metaphor from "The Texture of Time" (the fourth section of *Ada*) that becomes a constituent of the rest of the novel is the ardis (arrowhead) of time. In *Ada* it becomes Ardis Hall, the setting of the early sections. This transformation suggests that back of the love story that comprises the bulk of *Ada* lies a philosophical meditation on time.

The most recondite metaphor for time in "The Texture of Time" appears in the title of that chapter. Van means by texture something to which an artist can give pattern and vitality, making time more than the dull measuring rod brandished by realists. If it has texture it is interesting in itself instead of merely serving as a means to sort out events. Van thinks of this palpability when he says that he delights sensually in time (p. 406). This last notion provides the needed clarification for this metaphor, because it connects the idea of texture, the most important one in the essay, with the main action of the novel. The sex in the plot metaphorically represents sensual delight in time. In other words, caressing Ada stands for caressing time. Moreover, as the artist creates patterns and linguistic bliss in the novel he creates texture for the first time span that contains the novel's action. Most simply, then, *Ada*, this carefully fashioned artifact, is itself the texture of time.

Van also claims that time consists of the interval between events, not events themselves. He uses this idea to shape the plot, which he creates from the occasions when Van and Ada are together. These moments escape the clutches of time because they produce ecstasy; during them Van and Ada live a timeless existence like Adam and Eve in Paradise. The adversary relation of love and time appears dramatically in the aging that Ada goes through while she is separate from Van and in the fact that Van composes "The Texture of Time" in his mind while driving to meet her again and thereby end an interval.

Van's theory denies the traditional division of time into past, present, and future. He wonders if there has ever been a time when the past and the present were not clearly separate. Such a time does exist, in *Ada*, as Nabokov indicates by scrambling the time sequence in the history of the imaginary planet he describes in the novel. In this novel familiar sounding events occur in a temporal relationship to each other unlike the one described in history books. History, then, cannot reveal the past, because it is not a series of events that can be lined up on a continuum, but "a constant accumulation of images" (p. 413). Art, not history, deals in images. Taken literally, this theory explains the many references to painting in the novel and many of the other techniques, like the attempted avoidance of didacticism. In *Speak, Memory* Nabokov expresses the same theory of time in his image of the flashes of light, which represent moments of consciousness. Van claims that the third member of the traditional temporal series, the future, simply does not exist. Nabokov makes the same point in *Transparent Things*. This is a useful theory for novelists, since often they try to make an imaginary past seem like the present.

Nabokov manipulates genres to attack realism, thereby again exemplifying the Literature of Exhaustion. His most daring imitation of forms—imitating a critical edition in *Pale Fire* and turning philosophy into a novel in *Ada*—imply that the form of the novel has indeed been exhausted and that novels, if they are to be written at all, must now be written in other guises.

Nabokov most frequently develops the theme of time, and of course he does not accept the conventional notions of chronological and chronometric time that form the underpinnings of realistic fiction. Rather, he redefines time; in *Ada*, which contains his most significant development of this theme, he yearns to organize time for nonrealistic writers. To understand more fully the theme of time in *Ada*, it probably would be best to double back quickly to its appearance in *Lolita* and *Pale Fire*. The opening of *Lolita* seems to imply that Humbert desperately pursues his nymphet in order to recreate the timeless past of his childhood by recreating Annabel in Lolita. Julian Moynahan interprets Humbert's relation to time this way, and he goes on to place *Lolita* in a rich tradition in American literature—including *The Great Gatsby*—because of the way Nabokov handles this theme (p. 35). His analysis creates two problems: it plays into the hands of the Freudians, and the Poe allusions that describe Humbert's original timeless realm turn out to be false clues. Humbert does seek timelessness but the etiology of his childhood trauma should be ignored and his means of seeking timelessness emphasized. He tries to achieve timelessness first through his imaginative transformation of Lolita from a rather barbarous lttle girl into an icon, from pupa to butterfly. Thus, he accomplishes a watered-down version of an artistic transformation; but he also achieves the latter by narrating the book. In other words, he accomplishes two metamorphoses: changing Lolita from pupa to butterfly and changing the story of his first transformation from raw subject matter into art.

John Shade in *Pale Fire* also seeks timelessness, but his motives need to be examined; in fact, he insists on having them examined. Afraid that his fragile heart will give out, he tries in two ways to escape time. First, he strives to attain an eternal afterlife, a task at which he will probably fail, as indicated by his pathetic attempt to check his conception of eternity with someone else who seems to have the same conception. A long trip and a meeting with this other person end in disappointment when he learns that their apparent agreement resulted from a typographical error. His other method, creating poetry, has more promise, but, it, too, probably will not work for him. His kind of art, autobiographical poetry, does not lift him out of the stream of time; it thrusts him back into it. Furthermore, his motive taints his creative work because it turns that work to a nonaesthetic purpose.

Like Shade, Van Veen worries about his heart, not because he believes that it is flawed but because he believes that it has only so many beats in it and that each one brings him closer to the final one. Most of the time, though, he philosophically disposes of the problem of death. At the beginning of "The Texture of Time" he argues that death is irrelevant to the question of time, that it, euphemistically called "organic decline" and "unconsciousness," happens to things regardless of whether or not they are immersed in the flow of time. This argument does not convince; it merely reveals his fear of death. Next, however, he argues against the existence of a future time, which he does with greater cogency. This strategy, if it does not refute death, at least allows one to forget it for a while. Also, his strategy allows his other motives, which are aesthetic and therefore more impressive, to come to the fore.

Nabokov describes a lost timeless realm more fully in *Ada* than he does in *Lolita*. Ardis Hall exists outside of time, which the comparisons of it with Eden indicate. In the biblical version of an atemporal realm the onset of sexual awareness begins the time sequence, forcing Adam and Eve, following a burning brand, to leave their paradise of timelessness. The opposite happens in *Ada*, because the first sex act brings on a kind of timelessness for Van and Ada by making them invincible to mundane ravages like those of time. And the fire, a burning barn, conveniently removes possible spectators so that the two children can enjoy each other. They even in a sense escape God, because in *Ada* he is Log, the record of time.

Van also achieves timelessness by doing handstands, not such a ridiculous method, because "it [is] the standing of a metaphor on its head not for the sake of the trick's difficulty, but in order to perceive an ascending waterfall or a sunrise in reverse: a triumph, in a sense, over the ardis of time (p. 144–145). He uses this method only as a stopgap until he can learn to work with real metaphors: "Van on the stage was performing organically what his figures of speech were to perform later in life" (p. 145). He can use this more advanced method better than Humbert and Shade can, because he understands time more thoroughly and because he struggles against it for more purely aesthetic reasons.

One can defeat time also by turning away from the future to the past. If he can recapture the past and link it with the present, he can perceive time with perfect clarity and give the present moment the richest possible texture. Van accomplishes this, or has it accomplished for him, when Ada calls him after they had lost contact with each other for many years (p. 422). She is the past he has sought, not, as Humbert sought Annabel, in the guise of another or represented by someone whose reality he denies, but for herself and as she really is. He loves Ada in a way both aesthetically more sophisticated and emotionally more meaningful than Humbert loves Lolita.

Nabokov knows how hard the seeker of timelessness must strive. In *Speak, Memory* he talks about "the walls of time separating

[him] and [his] bruised fists from the free world of timelessness" (p. 14). He believes that humans inevitably will be obsessed with time. He even thinks that the dawn of consciousness coincides with the dawn of the sense of time (p. 14). But he has faith that he can attain timelessness, and not just by means of his art. Later in *Speak, Memory* he announces that he does not believe in time because he can evade it by observing butterflies.

Nabokov presents his theory of time in bits and pieces throughout his work, mainly in *Ada*, but when he reassembles it, it proves to be logical and of great use to a novelist. First, he assumes that the proper goal of an artist is to create timelessness; the realists err in thinking that they should recreate time by imitating real, or at least plausible, actions. He, but not the realists, can accomplish his goal because, although the intervals between events exist in time, events are timeless, if they have texture. If an artist adds texture to events, he will add vitality and meaning to them by shaping them aesthetically, putting them into patterns and describing them in all their complexity. Before he can add texture to a present event, it slips into the past, so he must call it up by means of memory, which connects past and present. Memory enables the imagination to work on the event and give it texture. An artist can easily make this retrieval, for the available past consists of images, the perfect raw material for the creative imagination.

Nabokov's attitude toward time differs slightly from Borges's. The latter flatly denies the existence of time, hypothetically of course. The former sometimes does the same but also sometimes argues for the existence of an alternative, artistic time. On the essential issue they agree, however, for even Nabokov's artistic time differs radically from the realists' time, which neither accepts.

Even in everyday terms time—the object—and memory—the storehouse—relate naturally to each other. Nabokov needs this natural connection since it makes art possible. In his essay on *Ada* in the *TriQuarterly* Appel over-states his point slightly but he is on the right track: "a Time caressing and caressed by the memory and imagination is the only medium for Nabokov's art" (p. 138). It is hard to know what Appel means by "medium," and attributing to time the ability to act on memory, instead of merely being acted on by it, contradicts both Nabokov's theories and his fiction. Appel, however, carefully chooses his metaphor of caressing, both for its accuracy and for its clarification of the sex in *Ada*.

An answer that Appel elicits in his interview with Nabokov, which appears in *Nabokov: The Man and His Work*, helpfully introduces Nabokov's theory of memory, because, despite its succinctness, it contains all the essential aspects of that theory:

> imagination is a form of memory. . . . An image depends on the power of association, and association is supplied and prompted by memory. When we speak of a vivid individual recollection we are paying a compliment not to our capacity of retention but to Mnemosyne's mysterious foresight in having stored up this or that element which creative imagination may use when combining it with later recollections and inventions. In this sense, both memory and imagination are a negation of time. (p. 32)

Here he describes the three main attributes of memory: its relation to the imagination, its ability to make patterns and its negation of time.

The first point is the crucial one because it provides the discriminations necessary to demonstrate that Nabokov's kind of memory differs from the realists' kind. The realists, depending heavily on ordinary conceptions of time, need memory to make that time available to them as subject matter. Because they trust in time's simplicity, they conceive of memory in the same way, as a mechanical tool for retrieving pieces of time. To them, memory operates like a fisherman setting up a net to span the stream of time and emptying it of its diverse, inchoate catch. Nabokov, however, does not believe that memory operates mechanically and indiscriminately. Hugh Person in *Transparent Things* can see back through time—a process like memory—when he looks at certain objects. Humbert lyrically addresses "Mnemosyne, sweetest and most mischievous of muses" (*Lolita*, p. 237). Like the imagination, Mnemosyne creates and selects. It is Nabokov's tenth muse, or his only one, with the familiar nine being merely avatars of it. It works like a sharp-eyed, deft person standing on the bank of time's stream, dipping his small net into it to catch only the right pieces.

The right pieces will form a pattern, a texture, as Van Veen argues in his "Texture of Time." Appel, in his *TriQuarterly* article, phrases it this way: "all the principles expounded in 'Veen's Time' are centered on the ability of memory to perceive Time as texture, rather than progression" (p. 141). This statement implies that the patterns exist at least potentially in time, and that a person need only see them with his memory—a difficult act that demands creative perception—rather than make them himself. This conception accords with one in *Speak, Memory*: "the supreme achievement of memory . . . is the masterly use it makes of innate harmonies when gathering to its fold the suspended and wandering tonalities of the past" (p. 126). This viewpoint must not be confused with the realists', who do not try to find patterns in remembrances. A specific illustration of the differences appears in the story in *Speak, Memory* of the Russian general who visited the Nabokov home when Vladimir was a boy. A messenger interrupted the simple trick with matches he was performing for the boy to tell him that he had been ordered to take command of Russian armies fighting the Japanese. Years later, when both the general and the Nabokovs were fleeing the revolution, the general, in disguise, asked Nabokov's father for a light. A realist discovering these two events would pounce on the irony, the historical implications, the change in social conditions, the exciting story line or the like. Nabokov was fascinated by the pattern in the match motif.

After a writer finds these potential patterns he must assemble them, at least in his imagination and, if possible, in an artistic creation. Julian Moynahan describes this step in the process when he claims that in *Speak, Memory* "things long dead and vanished in the past come fully to life precisely by being placed within a series of frames, by being 'reduced' or 'fixed' in a pattern, by being subdued to imagery and artifice" (p. 15). In this step of the process memory plays an active role, more so than it had in the previous step.

Memory also supplies the other ingredient of texture, vitality. Since memory deals with images, it adds vitality by coloring images, or by brightening the color that already exists. Again Humbert has the right idea. Recalling his "affair" with Annabel, he says of one image, "the arabesques of lighted windows . . . touched up by the colored inks of sensitive memory, appear to me now like playing cards" (p. 16). This description of the creative way his memory works should be enough to refute the Freudian interpretation of the effect his experiences with Annabel had on his later life. The same concept of memory's vitalizing function also appears in *Ada*, where Nabokov compares memory to Rembrandt painting exquisitely colored portraits of a remembered person (p. 85).

If the first two features of memory are present, the third inevitably appears. That is, if memory, first, creates, like the imagination, and second, if it discovers and vitalizes patterns, then it will defeat time. Memory can achieve its ultimate triumph by subsuming time so completely for its own advantage that time effectively becomes nonexistent. Then the remembering artist can announce, with Van Veen, "time is but memory in the making" (*Ada*, p. 425). Memory then does not serve time, as it does for a realist; it masters time.

The fact that Humbert defeats time through creative use of memory means that his experience with Lolita does not merely repeat an earlier experience, which is another possible way to refute time. Nabokov, unlike Borges, does not use this latter strategy. He could also use his invention in *Ada* of an imaginary world with a history of its own to create repetitions, but he does not develop any obvious examples, preferring instead to use this situation to scramble time. Nor is the example of the matches in *Speak, Memory* a Borgesian repetition. In it Nabokov emphasizes the role of memory in both spotting a resemblance and describing differences between the two events.

Nabokov works much less with the theme of space than he does with the theme of time. He brings it into his books occasionally, however, to show that commonsense ideas are mistaken. He creates a purely imaginative country, Zembla, in *Pale Fire* to attack space, but only mildly. Kinbote, Zembla's creator, uses an old strategy, merely adding facts so that Zembla resembles Slavic countries closely enough to make this invention seem almost realistic like, say, Hardy's Wessex. Nabokov sets *Lolita* in a painfully familiar America and conventionally uses the spatial setting in this novel. Only in *Ada* does he make a determined effort to disrupt his readers' ideas about space. On Terra countries of our world combine and mix in what appears to be an émigrée's view of geography. For example, Kaluga's waters are near Ladore, which from other references like Bryant's Castle (Chillon) can be recognized as equivalent to Lake Geneva, on which Nabokov now lives. But its sound associates it with two other places in the author's life, Lake Cayuga —the waters of which are mentioned in the song of Cornell University, where he taught—and Luga, a town south of the Nabokov estate in Russia. This shuffling of space contributes less to the novel than does the transformation of ordinary space into artistic space by means of dozens of references to painters and descriptions of scenes as if they were paintings. These last two techniques are analogous to his transformation of ordinary time into artistic time.

In this novel he also turns the humour theory, a method of organizing space, to his own uses, perhaps trying to metamorphose it so that realism will lose another of the conceptions it depends on. As their names reveal, the four most important minor characters in *Ada* represent three of the primary elements of the humour theory. Lucette is air, since "lucere" in Latin means to shine. She dies in water, jumping from a boat to drown herself when she abandons hope of winning Van. Demon is fire, since the satanic associations of his name suggest hell fire, and he dies in the air, in a plane crash. Two sisters, Aqua and Marina, are water. Marina seems to be the one relevant to this scheme because she is cremated, subjected to fire, after her death. This relation between characters and the elements that kill them makes literal sense. The elements associated with the characters also fit their personalities. Lucette has an airy personality: unstable, moody, insubstantial. Demon is fiery: dynamic and vital. Marina is aqueous: lethargic and, as an actress, capable of sea changes. Nabokov makes these characters two-dimensional partly because he wants them to fulfill these symbolic functions.

The writers of the Literature of Exhaustion consider patterns bad because they impose limits, but Nabokov's opinion of them differs a little from Borges's. Both recognize the danger of patterns in life. An intricate pattern kills Charlotte Haze: the conjunction of her distraction caused by her discovery of Humbert's diary, the presence of a dog that chases cars, and a car whose driver swerves into her to miss the dog. Humbert's most vivid realization of a pattern occurs when Lolita tells him that it was Quilty who stole her from him and he begins to reconstruct the clues that should have enabled him to discover this for himself. Despite his shock he responds more strongly to the pattern of the clues than to the identification of the villain: "quietly the fusion took place, and everything fell into order, into the pattern of branches that I have woven throughout this memoir with the express purpose of having the ripe fruit fall at the right moment" (p. 248).

Patterns are just as dangerous, though less obviously so, in *Pale Fire*. They intrigue Shade; he sometimes goes so far as to believe that only they have meaning. In his poem he writes:

> But all at once it dawned on me that *this*
> Was the real point, the contrapuntal theme;
> Just this: not text, but texture; not the dream
> But topsy-turvical coincidence,
> Not flimsy nonsense, but a web of sense.
>
> (p. 44)

But he, too, dies to complete a pattern. His murder occurs because of the convergence of a criminal, his own resemblance to the judge who sentenced the criminal and the movement of Kinbote from the judge's house to visit Shade. Shade makes the lethal error of failing to distinguish between patterns in life and in art. The artist can properly bring together real things to form a pattern, adding his own touch to the composition, but he should not expect ready-made patterns in life; this can be lethal.

Patterns that shock or destroy the characters have an entirely different effect if they are considered to be the author's creation. Actually, the author provides the clues to Quilty's identity, sets in motion the forces that will kill Charlotte Haze and Shade, and puts all the other patterns in his work. From this viewpoint patterns perform a useful function, making undeniable the author's presence in his book. Appel, in *The Annotated Lolita*, says, "Nabokov's passion for chess, language, and lepidoptery has inspired the most elaborately involuted patterning in his work. Like the games implemented by parody, the puns, anagrams, and spoonerisms all reveal the controlling hand of the logomachist" (p. xxviii). Nabokov's method of writing—composing on index cards and moving back and forth from part to part of the manuscript instead of writing it in the order in which it will be printed—makes it easier for him to establish such patterns. It may also partly cause the rare woodenness in his work, for instance in parts of *Pnin*. These patterns make his books seem completely under the control of the artist and suggest that only the artistic imagination can understand and control the world. In *Transparent Things* the characters continuously encounter nearly complete patterns. The large number of such patterns suggests that the master pattern-maker, Nabokov, has contrived the story. In regard to patterns, Nabokov's books have little in common with, say, Vermeer's paintings, which focus a viewer's attention on the Dutch burghers and other subjects represented in them. His books are more like Mondrian's paintings, which focus attention on patterns, and ultimately on the maker of these patterns.

Nabokov, like Borges, often uses death as a sign that a character has taken an incorrect position. Shade, besides his position on patterns, errs about another issue, the validity of autobiographical art, a mistake for which he deserves punishment. The well known opening of his poem is:

> I was the shadow of the waxwing slain
> By the false azure in the windowpane.
>
> (p. 23)

The bird he describes dies because it mistakes a reflection for an extension of space. Similarly, Shade dies because he creates reflecting and finite art. That is, he writes autobiographical poetry, reflecting himself in his work, rather than creating more possibilities. Kinbote deserves less blame on these grounds, even though he interprets Shade's poem to fit his own life. The vital difference is that Kinbote creates an imaginary "autobiography" and thus is not bound by anything that has happened; Shade creates a real, and thus limited, autobiography.

Thus, Borges and Nabokov basically agree about these themes that they consider negative. Borges dismisses out of hand the conventional opinions about time, memory, space, and patterns in life and goes on to deny the existence of these things. Nabokov also disagrees with the conventional notions but he redefines these concepts so that they will be usable for the Literature of Exhaustion. His redefinitions are so thorough that his position ends up very similar to Borges's, certainly similar enough to warrant placing the works of both in the Literature of Exhaustion.

Borges and Nabokov agree even more closely about the things they believe in. For example, they concur that an imaginary world can replace the supposedly real world. During the first stage in this process they mix the "real" and the imaginary so thoroughly that they become indistinguishable. In *Ada* science, logically enough, represents the "real" world. In this novel Ada is the scientist, Van the artist. Appropriately a character named Demon sires both these characters, which indicates that they can merge, for a demon, or daimon, has been thought to be the creative spirit that produces both art and science. Demon points out that the real and imaginative worlds overlap: "how incestuously . . . art and science meet in an insect, in a thrush, in a thistle of that ducal bosquet" (p. 332). Art and science do meet in this novel. Ada always has some artistic interests, especially in poetry and language in general, and she becomes less scientifically inclined as the book proceeds. Conversely, Van becomes more scientific as he turns his attention to the problem of time. The two disciplines combine in a more interesting way by means of the literally incestuous relationship of Van and Ada and their merging into "Vaniada." As their relationship proceeds, the "real" world seems to fade, it becomes clearer that they narrate the story and the omniscient narrator slowly disappears. That is, they combine into a story-telling demon.

Humbert transforms a girl who should be unattractive to him and to other adult males into an irresistible object, thus replacing reality even more completely than anyone in *Ada* does. Humbert most successfully transforms Lolita through his imagination when she plays tennis. He says that "her tennis was the highest point to which I can imagine a young creature bringing the art of make-believe, although I daresay, for her it was the very geometry of basic reality" (p. 211). He has an easy time transforming her then because her game is pure form. She moves lithely and with almost perfect grace, but her content is bad: she invariably loses. Humbert worships the form, seeing its latent patterns, and therefore the latent nymphet beneath the surface of the bobby-soxer. The appearance of a butterfly, for Nabokov a symbol of ecstasy and itself the metamorphosed pupa, marks the high point of his rapture.

Much less obviously, to some extent Van similarly transforms Ada. In all mental and emotional aspects Ada is tremendously superior to Lolita, but her physical attributes are not particularly attractive even in her youth and especially after she ages. The young Ada looks like this to her mother: "her hair was drawn back from her big round brow and thickly pigtailed. The rose of a rash under her lower lip glistened with glycerine through the patchily dabbed-on powder. She was too pale to be really pretty. . . . My eldest [Ada] is rather plain but has nice hair, and my youngest [Lucette] is pretty, but foxy red" (p. 101). Ada overpoweringly attracts Van, however, because he imaginatively transforms her.

Kinbote's imagination works even more efficiently than Humbert's and Van's. He can transmute not just one little girl but his whole life, imagining himself to be an exiled king and creating for himself a kingdom complete with subjects, palaces, a landscape, would-be regicides and brave monarchists. A reader should not dismiss his achievement as madness, to which the artist's work sometimes bears a slight resemblance. Shade, who understands the mixture of reality and imagination in Kinbote's mind, answers this charge: " 'That is the wrong word. . . . One should not apply it to a person who deliberately peels off a drab and unhappy past and replaces it with a brilliant invention" (p. 169).

But neither Humbert nor Kinbote literally creates art, the supreme replacement for the "real" world, and Shade does not create it in the highest sense, since his autobiographical art has notable deficiencies. For contrast with these major characters and for use as measuring rods by which they can be evaluated, Nabokov sprinkles his work with real artists. They include the invisible painters who take over in *Ada*, turning a scene into a painting and almost turning a page of print into a richly colored canvas; for example, "a moment later the Dutch took over: Girl stepping into a pool under the little cascade to wash her tresses, and accompanying the immemorial gesture of wringing them out by making wringing-out mouths—immemorial too" (p. 113).

Nabokov himself is the master artist, and sometimes he allows his readers to see his brush daubing paint on his canvas. Two pages from the end of *Ada* he comments that if Van and Ada die they will do so into the finished book (p. 443). A reader, previously caught in the book's spell, suddenly realizes, because of this remark, that these two characters are not real but fictional. Humbert cries out for such a reaction by the reader: "Imagine me; I shall not exist if you do not imagine me," which also rudely breaks the illusion. Nabokov makes the same point differently in *Pale Fire* when he tells the reader that he will observe the path of Gradus through the poem, "following the road of its rhythm, riding past in a rhyme, skidding around the corner of a run-on, breathing with the caesura, swinging down to the foot of the page from line to line as from branch to branch" (p. 56). That is, this character moves as the poem does, and the two become roughly equivalent. But of course the man and the trip are fictional, too. In this instance one can distinguish three planes of reality: Gradus's trip, that trip transformed into poetry, and that transformation described in the novel. Nabokov gets the reader to watch the relation between the first and the second and perhaps thereby to forget that this fictional world is fictional. The master conjurer has caught the reader watching the wrong hand.

Unlike Borges, Nabokov does not propose that life is a dream. He has some trouble developing this theme, because he has to fend off the Freudians with one hand so he has only one hand left to delineate his own theory of dreams. In *Transparent Things* he makes fun of Freudian psychology in a long section about dreams. He handles this subject most cogently in a brief passage in *Ada* (pp. 273–276). There he answers Freud by claiming that the improbabilities in dreams have little significance; they merely indicate that a person's mind works less rationally when he dreams than it does when he is awake. Nabokov also, in the person of Van, denies dream symbolism as well as other kinds of symbolism and will admit the validity only of metaphors. On the positive side, Van says that the two most interesting kinds of dreams are the erotic and the professional. Again *contra* Freud, he sees nothing remarkable in dreaming about the sexual aspects of women who interest him. His professional dreams mix his roles of writer and dreamer; for example, phrases he has recently composed influence his dreams. This last notion is the closest Nabokov gets to Borges's position, but this analogy between art and dream differs a good deal from the other writer's extensive claims.

Nabokov's relative lack of interest in dreams accords with his relative lack of interest in idealism. Ada alludes to a tenet of this school of philosophy when she says that Van wishes to prove that

Terra's existence as a state of mind equals its actual existence (p. 203). Nabokov does a little to support this hypothesis by including fairly numerous details about Terra, which give it an air of reality. But Borges probably would insist that Terra exists, precisely because someone imagines it; he insists something like this in "The Circular Ruins." For a moment Humbert accepts idealism. Oddly, it occurs at the instant of his secret orgasm with Lolita on his lap, when he mentions that she is "safely solipsized" (p. 57). At the moment when his relation to her finally becomes physical he believes that it is purely mental. If he correctly analyzes this apparently physical case, life must indeed be a dream. But again, Nabokov does not insist, for he drops this idea immediately, and he certainly does not make it prominent in this novel. Humbert usually attributes reality to his world and its center, Lolita; he merely transmutes them imaginatively.

Because of its pervasiveness in Nabokov's work, another theme of the Literature of Exhaustion is difficult to isolate and describe. Nabokov argues again and again that reality is purely linguistic. His hundreds of puns and other bits of verbal magic call attention to language as language instead of letting it be a transparent medium through which a reader sees action. Baroque passages—most notably the beginning of *Ada*—have the same effect. He also seems like a man who knows all the words; the picture of him in the *TriQuarterly* contemplating *Webster's Unabridged* is marvelously apt. Readers have found and critics have mentioned many examples of these qualities, but one important instance seems to have been overlooked. In *Pale Fire* he clearly transposes the names of two proponents of the heroic couplet, making Wordsmith and Goldsworth, but this trick is more complicated. Nabokov hides a moral there, too: the worker with words is worth gold. Humbert's cry "I have only words to play with" makes a fine summary of Nabokov's attitude on this subject—if one removes the "only," for, just perhaps, words are everything.

Critics have almost sufficiently analyzed the crucial theme of metamorphosis. It appears most prominently in *Lolita*. The butterfly imagery in this novel and elsewhere is the most interesting example. Diana Butler tries to trace the lepidoptery theme in *Lolita*, an interesting project, but Nabokov claims that she knows too little about the subject.[14] In *The Annotated Lolita* Appel indicates the importance of the metamorphosis theme in this novel: "crucial to an understanding of *Lolita* is some sense of the various but simultaneous metamorphoses undergone by Lolita, H. H., the book, the author, and the reader, who is manipulated by the novel's game-element and illusionistic devices to such an extent that he too can be said to become, at certain moments, another of Vladimir Nabokov's creations" (p. 340). If anyone has written a modern version of Ovid's *Metamorphoses* it is Nabokov, and he has done it for an involuted purpose: to argue against the world view of the realists. If the world continually changes guises, or can be made to do so by a writer of the Literature of Exhaustion, a realist cannot describe it, much less explain it. It will take an equally Protean art to explain it, an art that, with puns and other verbal and technical tricks, transforms itself constantly before the eyes of the reader. The brightly colored kaleidoscopic world of Nabokov's fiction does exactly that.

This theme of transformation pervades his work and subsumes two other themes that Borges keeps distinct. One is process; a world full of transforming objects always changes. The theme of opposites appears somewhat more independently in Nabokov's works, but often these opposites merge, like the artistic Van and the scientific Ada, in incest, or one of the opposites changes into the other, and this theme fades away. In either case the pairs of opposites in his work do not remain stable, which chips away at another cornerstone of realism because it contradicts one of realism's most important modes of thought: dialectics.

Besides artist-layman and realist-nonrealist, Nabokov also contrasts adult and childlike modes of thought. The splendor of the child's dreamlike world more closely resembles the artist's world and is thus superior to adult thought. The most idyllic scenes in *Ada* appear early in the book and describe Van and Ada's childhood at Ardis Hall. Despite their precocity, they see things then through the eyes of children. They try to prolong this existence, and after they, inevitably, lose it, they try to recapture it. Humbert, too, wants to return to his childhood. To Stegner this is the most important aspect of *Lolita*, which "is finally a moving story of ape-Humbert in his prison of impossible love (a love . . . for a lost childhood, resurrected for him by nymphets)" (p. 103).

Nabokov, however, does not yearn for childhood in itself. Rather, he wants the opportunity to remember a past time, indeed a past that he did not completely understand when he experienced it. Such malleable material attracts an artist. Even Humbert recognizes this. He admits that during his childhood Annabel was not a nymphet; she became one only after twenty-nine years of remembering have shaped his recollection of her (p. 19). Remembrance of things past is also one of the central experiences in Nabokov's own life. Neither the financial nor political implications of the Russian Revolution make that event disastrous for him. He mourns the premature ending of his childhood. However, he has learned to turn this misfortune into an advantage. In *Speak, Memory* he says, "the nostalgia I have been cherishing all these years is a hypertrophied sense of lost childhood, not sorrow for lost banknotes" (p. 54). His phrasing is significant, for he says that he cherishes his sense of childhood. "Cherishing" is of course positive, and his *sense* of his childhood, not that childhood itself, attracts him.

Childhood's timelessness also makes it joyous. Children too young to be fully conscious live in a timeless world, and so do slightly older children, for their values do not usually include time. Stegner believes that Humbert, in searching for his lost years, searches "for the timeless, immortal, uncomplicated, never-never land in which preadolescents seem to live, rather than [has] an obsession with the physically real little girl" (p. 111). Thus, during childhood some of Nabokov's values such as dreams, imagination, and timelessness reign, so it provides some of the most pleasant material for memory.

Sex, like childhood, provides an attractive escape from the everyday existence in which realists immerse themselves. To prove this

Nabokov must refute the man who has preempted the topic and enraged him: Freud. Nabokov detests Freud mainly for arguing that not an artist but something else, such as sex, causes art. In *Lolita* he bluntly counters Freud: "sex is but the ancilla of art" (p. 236). He presents as evidence this book itself, proof, first, that art can subordinate sex to its own purposes, using it for instance to develop themes like memory and metamorphosis. *Lolita* also demonstrates that an artist, if he has enough skill, can describe sexual eccentricities or any other seemingly taboo subject so as to make them at least acceptable to a reader, and perhaps even make the reader see beauty in the descriptions of them. He also uses other methods to make sexual peculiarities acceptable in a novel. For example, he makes them symbolic in order to deflect attention from the sex itself to its meaning in the book. Ironically, Freud recognized that this often happened to sex. He uses this method with both Kinbote's homosexuality and Humbert's nymphetomania. Both characters are aliens, Europeans in America, and their sexual anomalies, among other things, symbolize the alien's loneliness. They desire sexual objects that they have trouble attaining, thus isolating themselves, just as the alien inevitably lives to some extent in isolation.

The incest in *Ada* is a bit more complicated than the sexual variations in the other two books. At one point in *Ada* Nabokov says that incest is taboo because it interferes with human evolution (p. 107). He does not mean this to be the final explanation, for it sounds like a realist's evaluation. In his *TriQuarterly* article, Appel argues that the incest in this novel represents Nabokov's "abiding devotion to Russian, the dazzling infidelities which exile has forced on him, and the unique intimacy he has achieved with his own writings as begetter, translator, and re-translator" (p. 124). His third point makes sense but is quite trivial because in *Ada* Nabokov rarely mentions, or makes relevant, his other work, and his translations of his own work form a relatively unimportant part of his artistic accomplishment. A language seems like an odd incestuous partner, and if Russian were such a partner, why is English not one also? I can see no possible meaning in the phrase about Nabokov's "dazzling infidelities." The incest motif has a much less exotic and more precise meaning than the one Appel cites. It symbolizes, as I have mentioned, the relation between the scientific and artistic parts of Nabokov's sensibility.

In *Ada* sex, as the combination of art and science and the attainment of timelessness, is truly real, and therefore unlike the false reality of the realists. Van believes that "in his love-making with Ada he discovered the pang, . . . the agony of supreme 'reality.' Reality, better say, lost the quotes it wore like claws" (p. 169). Nabokov treats sex more frankly in *Ada* than he does in *Lolita*, but he still uses it as a metaphor. He thus develops this staple theme of realistic fiction in a way consistent with his other themes and techniques.

In summary, Borges and Nabokov have similar values, but they place different emphases on them. For example, Borges is more interested in idealism, Nabokov in metamorphosis. Borges also deals more discursively with these topics, partly because he has written more essays than Nabokov, partly because he writes more philosophical fiction. Nabokov often admits the existence of some kind of real world, although he quickly transforms or redefines it. Borges hesitates to grant even this much status to "reality." Thus, as they did with their negative themes, they similarly develop their positive themes. It still seems clear that Nabokov and Borges can best be understood by considering them together as writers of the Literature of Exhaustion.

They also both depend most heavily on images to make their points. Their theories of literature suggest that they should do this. A realist would most often use the elements that play a larger part in man's everyday experiences, like character and action, but Nabokov mainly uses a more purely literary element. He has revealed that in the early works, which he wrote under the pseudonym Sirin, "the real life . . . flowed in his figures of speech" (*Speak, Memory*, p. 213). In his book on Gogol he explains how that writer depended on his figures of speech, comparing inanimate objects with people and thus, by means of a brilliant condensation, indirectly populating his book. Nabokov does not want to draw a comprehensive picture of society, as Gogol did, so he uses his images and figures of speech differently, though just as extensively.

Van remarks in his lecture on dreams that objects can have only metaphoric relationships, never symbolic ones, a theory with which Nabokov agrees (p. 277). Nabokov has repeatedly scoffed at symbolic interpretations of his work, claiming that he merely describes. He of course is not as rigorous about this as he claims; at least one can convincingly attach symbolic meanings to some of his images. In the three novels that belong to the Literature of Exhaustion he shares one recurrent image, the mirror, with Borges, but he rarely uses circles and labyrinths. Instead of the latter two, his other dominant image is the butterfly.

The meanings of his mirror imagery change from book to book. Although some of the many mirrors in *Lolita* have no symbolic meaning, they appear in crucial passages to add an air of strangeness and thereby to make the action seem even more important. Quilty's house is full of mirrors, the most eerie ones being in one room that contains little else except a polar bear rug (p. 268). The hotel room in which Humbert and Lolita first sleep together has an incredible number of mirrors: "there was a double bed, a mirror, a double bed in the mirror, a closet door with mirror, a bathroom door ditto, a blue-dark window, a reflected bed there, the same in the closet mirror" (p. 110). Thus, in *Lolita* Nabokov uses a typical symbol of the Literature of Exhaustion but does not attach to it meanings characteristic of that literature; in fact he attaches almost no meaning at all to it.

By the time he wrote *Pale Fire* he had concluded that mirrors copy reality either accurately or falsely and, as a nonrealist, he had begun to prefer inaccurate copying. Both of the main characters live in a world of mirrors. Kinbote explains that Zembla is a "land of reflections, of 'resemblers' " (p. 187). That is, the mirror in which he sees it is not accurate—if it were, the image would be an exact copy, not a resemblance—because his imagination has produced

Zembla. Two pages later he mentions the mirror of exile, which explains the impetus for his fantasy. "Fantasy" in this instance needs to be stripped of its negative connotations, because according to this novel imaginative creation is better than copying.

Unlike Kinbote, Shade tries to copy accurately. The first two lines of his poem indicate the danger of mirrors, because reflections kill the waxwing: his name is almost identical with the name of the revolutionary group, the Shadows, that kills Shade (according to Kinbote's version of his death). Besides the similarity in sound, "shade" and "shadow" both refer to dark patterns "reflected" from objects. Mary McCarthy points out another reflection involving Shade and the member of the organization who kills him. "Gradus" is Russian for degree, which in turn is a synonym of "shade" (p. 74). Nabokov drops other hints that the killer mirrors his victim: the occupations of Gradus, glazier, and the man with his "mirror name," Sudarg of Bokay, a mirror manufacturer. Shade would have been safer had he not tried to mirror his life accurately in his work, but he dies in the wilderness of mirrors in which he lives.

The accurate mirror of realism appears also in *Ada*. In one instance a character uses it not to confuse but to cheat at cards. However, Van wins the game because his sleight of hand tricks are the work of an illusionist and thus superior to any realistic tricks with mirrors. At one point Nabokov explicitly conveys the meaning that he finally attaches to accurate mirrors. Mlle Lariviere writes realistic fiction, reproducing works by De Maupassant. Nabokov reveals in a description the nature and value of her work: "behind the samovar (which expressed fragments of its surroundings in demented fantasies of a primitive genre)" (p. 75).

Nabokov concludes "On a Book Entitled *Lolita*" with an image of the illusionist, whose trick mirror represents nonrealistic art. He modestly, and undoubtedly ironically, laments that switching from Russian to English has left him "devoid of any of those apparatuses —the baffling mirror, the black velvet backdrop, the implied associations and traditions—which the native illusionist, frac-tails flying, can magically use to transcend the heritage in his own way" (p. 288).

Any illusionist would envy the nonrealistic mirror trick in *Ada*: the scene with Ada, Van, and Lucette in bed. Nabokov thus acknowledges two kinds of mirrors, one good and one bad. This position contrasts with the consistently negative evaluation of mirrors in Borges's work, and prepares for the fun-house mirrors in Barth's fiction.

In *Lolita*, *Pale Fire*, and *Ada* Nabokov develops the butterfly image even more extensively than the mirror image. In *Lolita* this image is completely positive, appearing in the tennis scene as a sign of Humbert's transformation of Lolita into an exquisite creature of his imagination. It also appears throughout this book in scattered allusions to the species of butterfly the female of which Nabokov discovered, though some of the interpretations of this image in Butler's "Lolita Lepidoptera" are perhaps incorrect. He uses this image to glorify the transformation of the real world into a better imaginative world.

In *Pale Fire* Nabokov attacks as too naive complete faith in the power of the imagination. Shade early in the novel can, like Humbert, create a figurative butterfly. The Vanessa he mentions is both a butterfly (the Red Admirable) and a beloved woman and subject of literature (Swift's Vanessa), and he equates her with his wife Sybil. But butterflies have an important quality, their patterns, in addition to their metamorphoses and their beauty. These patterns are negative because Shade finds, rather than creates, them. The completed pattern of his death is signalled by the appearance of a butterfly, appropriately another Vanessa. Kinbote's real name, Botkin, is once compared to "botfly," which sounds like "butterfly" but is a parasite, not a beautiful transformed creature. Kinbote could be like a butterfly, because in his fantasy of Zembla he has achieved a metamorphosis, but in order to tell his story he has to be parasitic on Shade's poem. In *Pale Fire* Nabokov suggests that butterflies are good insofar as they suggest metamorphosis, bad insofar as they suggest a pattern found in the real world instead of an invented pattern.

In *Ada* Nabokov even doubts the value of metamorphosis, as he shows by the way he uses the butterfly image. Ada likes larvae, insects that have not undergone metamorphosis, and she once goes so far as to kill a butterfly that has just metamorphosed (p. 53). She apparently feels that any change will be for the worse. She is twelve when she meets Van, the same age that Lolita was when Humbert met her, but Ada has already matured and she attracts Van; she needs no change. Two cross references to *Lolita* encourage a comparison between these two female characters. Early in *Ada* Nabokov mentions Lolita, Texas, and then describes Demon in butterfly terms, with crumpled wings. This scene takes place during torrential rains, like those that occurred during Nabokov's hunt for the butterfly he discovered. Another butterfly mentioned later, *Nymphalis carmen*, alludes to the earlier book because of the comparisons between Lolita and Carmen. Ada wisely fears change. The reference to the *Nymphalis carmen* occurs at a major change in Ada's life, her first parting with Van, and after this scene Nabokov makes no more butterfly references. He replaces them with references to insect pests like mosquitoes and flies. The butterfly images in *Ada* suggest that one cannot depend on being happy with the changes he can make, even artistic ones, if he uses the real world as raw material. It follows from this idea that it may be better for the artist to turn his back on reality and create self-enclosed work.

Nabokov's characterization creates just such a self-enclosed artistic domain. All his major characters in these three books are readers or writers or both. Humbert writes his memoirs, which comprise *Lolita*; Lolita fits less neatly into these categories than the other characters, but Humbert does occasionally mention what she reads, and he lists the books he buys for her. Kinbote writes the notes and Shade the poem in *Pale Fire*, and the poem contains many allusions to Shade's reading. Van and Ada collaborate to write *Ada*, with the former doing most of the work, and a reader learns about many of the prodigious number of books they read. Hugh Person in *Transparent Things* is either, or both, an editor and a character in the novels written by Mr. R.

The disguises in these books dispute the commonsense idea that characters, like real people, have well established identities. They also become more prevalent as Nabokov progresses from *Lolita* to *Pale Fire* to *Ada*. In the first of these novels Humbert avoids disguise, and Lolita uses it only once, and then in a not very literal sense, in her role in the play. Quilty masterfully disguises himself, both during his chase of Humbert and Lolita and during his escape with her. The pseudonyms he invents for motel registers are a good example. Shade is what he appears to be, but Kinbote is really Botkin in disguise and he tells a story about a king who escaped in disguise. Kinbote pretends to be that king. He disguises himself so artfully that it takes a while for the reader to guess his identity. In *Ada* all the major characters disguise themselves, so a reader can use none of them as a touchstone to find the truth. Ada, like her mother, is an actress and plays more stage roles than Lolita's one role. Van assumes the disguise of Mascodagama for a vaudeville act. The confusion about the family relation between Van and Ada can also be considered a disguise, and it creates at least as difficult a puzzle as the identity of the narrative voice in *Lolita*.

The double theme appears prominently in all three books despite Nabokov's claim that he has created no real doubles in his work (*Nabokov: The Man and His Work*, p. 37). It, too, intensifies from *Lolita* to *Pale Fire* to *Ada*. In *Lolita* it is important only in the confrontation between Humbert and Quilty, where Nabokov treats it comically, as a spoof of the double convention in fiction. The well known struggle for the gun is the broadest comedy: "I rolled over him. We rolled over me. They rolled over him. We rolled over us" (p. 272). Alfred Appel puts *Lolita* in a tradition with other novels that have the double theme and argues that this novel contains allusions to other works in that tradition (p. lxiv). He bases some of his arguments on trivial resemblances, like references to the double as a shadow, and he sometimes oversimplifies; for example, the references to apes, as Appel says, refer to Poe's "William Wilson," but they also refer to the seed that grew into this novel, the story of the ape who learned to draw the bars of his cage. Appel's main idea, however, has merit.

Besides the double relation of Shade and Gradus, two others appear in *Pale Fire*. A minor one involves two unimportant Zemblans, Odon and Nodo. Hazel Shade, the poet's daughter, and Kinbote are lonely people who have trouble relating to the opposite sex, the former because of her shyness and unattractive appearance, the latter because of his homosexuality. In compensation for their loneliness they seek a more attractive world. Hazel becomes interested in psychic phenomena and finally settles not for a better world but for the oblivion of suicide. Kinbote compensates by creating his fantasy of Zembla and by hoping that Shade will write about him. Ironically, Kinbote's double, not he, plays a major role in "Pale Fire," and Kinbote never sees their similarity.

In *Ada* the double theme occupies a central place, since the two main characters are doubles. Robert Alter calls them the "two complementary halves of one self," which makes them like the androgynes in the story Aristophanes tells in *The Symposium*.[15] Alfred Kazin thinks that Ada is the double of Nabokov's scientific self, Van of his artistic self.[16] Both critics are right. The fact that Van and Ada are the doubles of Nabokov explains their negative features, since one member of a pair of doubles should be evil (this point makes Hazel and Kinbote less than an ideal pair of doubles, since both are pathetic rather than truly evil). Van has a prominent streak of cruelty that justifies his last name. "Veen" is the transliteration of the Russian word for cruelty. Ada makes a suitable pun on her own name: "iz ada" means out of hell. By creating these characters Nabokov considers the possible shortcomings of his two avocations.

Plot, a staple of realistic fiction, forms the grid into which most authors place the action. It annoys Nabokov, however, so he does what he can to eliminate it. If plot is defined quite tightly as, say, a sequence of events ordered by cause and effect relations, *Pale Fire* has no plot since it is just a poem with commentary and index. Even in *Speak, Memory*, where he writes about events that happened in a sequence, he loops forward and backward in time instead of always going forward in a straight line. In his novels he sometimes mocks readers who expect an orderly plot. For example, in *Ada* he includes a number of stock scenes at appropriate points, but he presents them tongue-in-cheek and when they are over he goes back to the rambling narrative that he prefers. Robert Alter lists the trite scenes: "the young man's return to the ancestral manor, the festive picnic, the formal dinner, a midnight blaze on the old estate, the distraught hero's flight at dawn from hearth and home as the result of a misunderstanding, the duel, the hero's profligacy in the great metropolis" (p. 48). Nabokov also toys with the reader by dropping hints about future action. Some are false, like the *Carmen* allusions in *Lolita*; others true, like the jingle "Guilty of killing Quilty." The reader, not knowing which hints to trust, should learn not to expect logical plots.

Finally, he attacks conventional notions of plot by creating numerous coincidences to show that the author, not the logic of events, determines what comes next. Nabokov recognizes the implications of the "dazzling coincidences that logicians loathe and poets love" (*Lolita*, p. 31). The logician depends on a universe subject to identifiable laws, but Nabokov will not affirm that such a universe exists. In *Ada* Van taunts the logicians and other realists about the coincidences that perplex them: "some law of logic should fix the number of coincidences, in a given domain, after which they cease to be coincidences, and form, instead, the living organism of the new truth" (p. 275). Thus, Nabokov uses coincidences, too, to show that he prefers the patterns in art to the patterns in life.

Carl Proffer on his *Keys to Lolita* has made a substantial analysis of Nabokov's style, so a repetition is hardly in order. It will be useful, however, to develop a bit further one of Proffer's insights. He claims, on the basis of a good deal of evidence, that the style of *Lolita* is "sound-determined" (p. 93). This feature makes Nabokov's work seem more poetic than fictional. More relevant to this study, it shows that a writer who determines his style on the basis of sound will value literary connections, not the connections he finds in the world. D. Barton Johnson has explained in detail

Nabokov's use of sound.[17] Thus, Nabokov's style is one of his most subtle arguments for the Literature of Exhaustion's positions, because it works almost imperceptively on the reader.

The style of "Pale Fire" imitates Pope and Wordsworth, Nabokov being as skilled a mimic as some of the butterflies he admires for this gift. If a poet needs to mimic earlier poets, a reader suspects that poetry has been exhausted. In order to highlight this conclusion Nabokov makes Shade's style less vital and noticeable than Humbert's. Nabokov has gracefully written the notes, however; despite his laments about being forced to write in an alien tongue, he seems incapable of clumsiness. Furthermore, a mundane style would be too much like the style of the workaday world, which he tries to escape.

The style of the opening of *Ada* differs considerably from his style elsewhere. Its turgidity has undoubtedly discouraged many readers. Some people preferred not to read about "that tesselated protectorate still lovingly called 'Russian' Estoty, which comingles, granoblastically and organically, with 'Russian' Canady" (p. 13). The prose becomes less thick later, but Nabokov attacks a reader who has made it through to page 381, because of the reader's earlier reservations about his style. In a passage addressed to Van but applicable to himself also, Nabokov advises writers to laugh at "cretinic critics, especially lower-upper-middle-class Englishmen [who] accuse his turnstyle of being 'coy' and 'arch' " (p. 381). This novel's beginning seems to be designed to drive away everyone but his proper audience, and he admonishes this saving remnant not to forsake the faith. He wants readers able to tolerate the baroque opening and therefore able to appreciate the beauties of the style in which he has written most of the book. They should revel in this style for itself, not demanding querulously that they be given the larger dose of plot and characterization that they get from realistic novelists.

Point of view has more importance in Nabokov's work than in Borges's. *Lolita* is quite conventional in this regard, but *Pale Fire,* because of its combination of poem and commentary and its narrator's weak grasp of reality, is more distinctive. In *Ada* Van and Ada both narrate, the point of view alternates from third-person to first-person, and the amount of knowledge the narrator has varies. More important, the authorial voice frequently asserts its independence from the character who is narrating. This happens in *Ada*, for example, when the voice says that neither Van nor Ada can adequately describe a scene, though the voice could do so if it wanted to (p. 298). Similarly, the narrator sometimes discloses knowledge that he could not possibly have. In these ways Nabokov breaks the illusion, revealing that he does not create a transparent medium through which the reader sees the world, but an opaque medium meaningful in itself.

Nabokov's work is more evidently comic than Borges's. Like Borges, he uses academic humor: satire directed at other writers and at intellectual projects, comic allusions and other jokes, all of which take some knowledge to appreciate. Laymen can more easily understand the humor in *Lolita*, and the interplay between Humbert's wit and his despair creates an effective tension. Even the dandyism of *Ada* can be funny to someone with enough tolerance, or to another dandy. This humor balances, without negating, his serious themes and makes it hard for the reader to despair about the death of the novel. The hours of silvery laughter reading him in the study more than balance the hours spent in dusty libraries tracking down his allusions.

He contrasts all of these features from the Literature of Exhaustion in his work with the conventional theme of love. In *Lolita* he ambiguously develops this theme. One of the key statements about it is that "mirage and reality merge in love," the announced message of the play within the novel. It is difficult to determine what the proportions of this mixture are, how much of Humbert's feeling for Lolita is based on mirage—the conception of her in his imagination, with all the implications for the aesthetic theme of the novel—and how much is really based on her. Mirage clearly dominates most of the book but the final meeting between Humbert and Lolita appears to be different. Andrew Field takes at face value Humbert's professions of love for the older, dowdy Lolita, and many other critics agree (p. 343). Julian Moynahan remains skeptical, admitting that Humbert "loves her *as she is*" but adding that Humbert "does not relinquish his habit of imaginary role playing," because he plays Don José to her Carmen (p. 33).

The burden of proof lies on the critics who do not accept Humbert's descriptions of his attitude, but they have strong evidence on their side. Moynahan argues convincingly about Humbert's roleplaying. This scene relates to the confrontation between Humbert and Quilty, and the obvious parody in that latter scene influences the meaning of the scene between Humbert and Lolita. The imagery, however, provides the best evidence, which is not surprising in Nabokov. Humbert describes the old Lolita as "the faint violet whiff and dead leaf echo of the nymphet I had rolled myself upon with such cries in the past; an echo on the brink of a russet ravine" (p. 253). He then claims to love her in all her substantiality, but soon he returns to his previous attitude, claiming that if her body decays he will still love "the mere sound of your raucous young voice, my Lolita" (p. 253). At the very end of the novel he recounts a mournful experience of his loss. The setting resembles the "russet ravine" on the brink of which she was the echo, and again her voice matters most to him: "I knew that the hopelessly poignant thing was not Lolita's absence from my side, but the absence of her voice from that concord" (p. 380). The voice is the most evanescent of qualities, the one most like a mirage. In the last sentence of the book, Lolita becomes a purely artistic object and loses all connection with reality: "And [art] is the only immortality you and I may share, my Lolita" (p. 281). Although love, in an etherialized form, occurs in *Lolita*, this voice imagery shows that the mirage in Humbert's love dominates the reality.

A reader should have less trouble understanding the love in *Pale Fire*. Mary McCarthy says that "love is the burden of *Pale Fire*. Love and loss" (p. 81). Although perhaps a bit too emphatic, this statement helpfully corrects the common tendency to ignore this theme in favor of the aesthetic themes in this work. Many readers slight this theme because its most notable examples occur in the poem, in which Shade describes his love for both his wife and his daughter.

In *Ada* love is both uncomplicated and obviously central. A pun underlines this point: the Veens are the children of Venus, a fact that nothing in the novel negates (p. 312). The increasing importance of the love theme in Nabokov's recent work, culminating in its manifestation in *Ada*, indicates that he may be moving away from the more purely artistic themes of the Literature of Exhaustion. Even if he does return to more conventional themes—such as love—however, he will not develop them realistically, for that would be to renounce both his own past work and his connection with the literary movement described here.

As to an evaluation of his work, the charge of repetitiousness that has been leveled against Borges does not apply to Nabokov. He is more inventive, does not use the artistically dangerous strategy of repetition to refute time and has shown some signs in *Ada* and *Transparent Things* of moving beyond the Literature of Exhaustion. Other detractors may argue that he limits himself to artistic matters, ignoring social and political issues. Albeit idiosyncratic ones, *Bend Sinister* and *Invitation to a Beheading* clearly are political books, and even his recent novels contain some social material. His concern in them is broader than aesthetics, and can more accurately be called epistemological, though he speculates mainly on how men know aesthetically. Epistemological issues have social consequences, since nearly all human actions depend on man's finding and organizing knowledge. But one need not argue on these grounds, because the same answer that should silence Borges's critics applies to Nabokov: he must be allowed to choose his subject matter.

After dealing with these general matters one can consider his contributions to various genres. It would take a critic fluent in Russian to evaluate his poetry in that language. The English poem he creates for Shade is better than competent; its quality has usually been rated too low. But he does not qualify as a major poet. *Speak,*

Memory belongs in the forefront of twentieth century autobiography, partly for his original use of imagery in it and partly for its haunting evocation of a fascinating life. Judging from his *obiter dicta* on other writers and reports of his Cornell lectures, the book that will be made from these lectures could very well establish him as an important critic. His sharp eye and acid wit will certainly make him at least an interesting critic. His translation of *Eugene Onegin* is controversial but fascinating. Despite his theory that translations should be crabbed, much of his verse translation has real grace, and its notes are intriguing.

His novels represent his major work. Among the ones I have covered *Lolita* and *Pale Fire* are great, both for the daring originality of their conceptions—which advance the genre of the novel, especially in the case of the latter—and for the meticulous way Nabokov realizes these conceptions. *Ada* is also impressively conceived, but it falls short of the other two because of the high price paid for the point that its early thick style makes. According to information current about his projects there will be much, much more from him, for which readers can be hopeful.

If one considers all these works together, Nabokov belongs among the major living writers. His ability to use some of the techniques and themes of the Literature of Exhaustion without weakening the other aspects of his work demonstrates his literary ability. He also has created interesting variations on these techniques and themes, for instance his complicated use of mirror images and his handling of the theme of metamorphosis. He has had less recognition than he deserves, partly because of the difficulty of his works and partly because it has taken time for his early books written in Russian, which clarify his later works and add to his stature, to be translated. The problem of his nationality has also hurt his standing. American literature anthologies rarely include him, I trust for this reason, since his work certainly surpasses much of the material usually found in those books. Happily, his reputation is rising, and the quite high quality of the criticism of his work, along with his future books, will, one hopes, keep this momentum going.

John Barth

John Barth, a generation younger than Borges and Nabokov, has had the great advantage of beginning his writing career after those two older writers had published a considerable body of work from which he could learn. As his essay "The Literature of Exhaustion" demonstrates, he has used this advantage. However, he does not slavishly copy the other two. Unlike Borges and Nabokov, he has explained what they are doing. This evident self-consciousness—part of an infinite regress since it focuses on a self-conscious literature—has helped him to notice and to use in his fiction the most important landmarks in literary history that identify the path leading to the Literature of Exhaustion. He has also codified this kind of literature and even mapped the next steps that fiction can take.

Barth's first two novels, *The Floating Opera* (1956) and *The End of the Road* (1958), are quite conventional and realistic. In them the young Barth—he wrote them both during his twenty-fifth year —looked for his proper mode. He found a mode suitable enough for him to write two reasonably impressive novels, particularly *The Floating Opera*. Despite their intrinsic merit they do not fit into this study because they lie outside the Literature of Exhaustion. I will take some backward glances at them, however, because they lead logically to his later books.

These later works are *The Sot-Weed Factor* (1960), *Giles Goat-Boy* (1966), *Lost in the Funhouse* (1968), and *Chimera* (1972).[1] His four recent works are at first glance very different; colonial American history written in the form of an eighteenth century novel, a mythical account of a hero with various allegorical meanings adhering to it, a collection of bizarre short stories, and a collection of three novellas, two of them rewritten myths. However, the logical development of Barth's career in this phase, the many interrelations among these four works, and his relationships with Borges and Nabokov will soon become clear.

One can most quickly understand Barth's work, too, by looking at his use of Chinese boxes. In *The Sot-Weed Factor* his way of showing the complex and obscure relations between reality and imagination differs from Borges's and Nabokov's, for he mixes the two domains in each box rather than establishing a clear boundary for the whole series, with imagination on one side and reality on the other. Because an actual poem gives him the bare bones of his story, that poem as well as Barth himself are in the outermost box. Barth of course is real, and the poem is both real, because it exists in print, and imaginary, because his imagination has created it. *The Sot-Weed Factor* comes next and is likewise both real and imaginary. Then follows the most complex box and also the one that contains the infinite possibilities that the Literature of Exhaustion seeks: the historical and pseudo-historical material of the novel, including the journals of Burlingame and John Smith. These journals are real in that they describe historical people, conditions and events, but they are also imaginary since they do not exist outside this novel and since they contradict the conventional notions about colonial American history. The main plot line has the same status as the journals, except that its action has not been written down elsewhere, as the journals have been. The difference between the journals and the rest of the plot is not so great that another layer, containing Smith and Burlingame, must be added, for Smith and Burlingame did not really write these purely fictive journals. Lacking this easy way out—drawing another box—the reader confronts another snarl because he must try to decide about what is real, a problem that Barth wanted to create. Barth has thus vastly complicated the old problem of the relative reality of frame and main story. He could make this problem infinitely more complicated and could string this novel out to an infinite length, delaying the death of the novel as Scheherazade delayed her own death by using her inventiveness. A writer using Barth's method in *The Sot-Weed Factor* could write an infinitely long novel if he invented an infinite number of journals or an infinite number of actions that he can claim to be historical.

Of all the systems that the three writers have devised that of the boxes in *Giles Goat-Boy* most quintessentially suits the Literature of Exhaustion. When a reader finally works his way to the innermost box all the others seem to evaporate and Barth seems to have made out of nothing a novel of 766 pages. The first two boxes are the familiar ones of author and novel. Then comes the narrative and within it the various allegorical planes that the narrative produces. This novel has no allegorical *levels* like Dante's, with one level being more important than the others and each of them operating at every point in the story. Rather, Barth develops different subjects by means of allegory—history, psychology, etc.—but he does not work on all of them at any given point in the story and he does not make any of them more important than the others.

The next box contains two things that are more basic to the novel than the allegorical planes, which help explain them. One is a theme, the problem of absolutes, particularly whether or not they exist. The other component is an action, George's attempt to fulfill his assignment. These two components relate intimately to each other because each of the seven parts of the assignment depends on the successful handling of a pair of opposites, each member of which lays claim to being an absolute. It turns out that in the novel absolutes do not exist in any simple sense, which negates the allegory, because allegories depend on absolutes for significance and clarity. With the absolutes and the allegories discredited, the only meaningful material left is George's attempt to fulfill his assignment. But, startlingly, Barth never reveals whether or not George succeeds; this topic gradually fades out as if it, too, has no meaning. After its elimination only one substantial thing remains: another attempt to fulfill an assignment. Barth accomplishes his purpose of writing a novel, gradually shucking away all his material and leaving only the process of the writing. This sounds like Tony Tanner's notion of entropy, applied not to the world but to a novel. In other words, the subject matter of fiction appears to be exhausted so the narrative impulse must get along by itself, with the aid of the little impetus it gets from demonstrating that its material is used up. Some readers may feel swindled by Barth's negation of his story's significance. Others may admire his ingenuity.

In "Menelaiad," a story in *Lost in the Funhouse*, he surely sets the world record for Chinese boxes. Its tangle of quotation marks indicates the many stories within stories. For example, readers must make sense of punctuation like this:

" ' " ' " 'Why?' I repeated," I repeated,' (p. 148)

These are the boxes:

1. Barth
2. "Menelaiad"
3. Menelaus' voice
4. Menelaus' story of Telemachus' visit to him
5. Menelaus' story of himself and Helen at sea, told to Telemachus
6. Menelaus' story of Eidothea and Proteus, told to Helen
7. Menelaus' story of himself and Eidothea, told to Proteus
8. Menelaus' story of himself and Helen in Troy, told to Eidothea
9. Menelaus' story about why Helen ran off with Paris, told to her and told by someone in the third-person.

Because the subject of most boxes becomes the auditor of the next one, these boxes interlock, which is a new feature. This sequence stops in the last box because the subject of this box is also its auditor. In the last box the point of view changes to the third person, as if Menelaus fades out of the story. Barth does not identify the narrative voice that replaces him, which makes it seem more like a narrative impulse, trying to keep the story going despite the odds, than like a narrative voice. As in *Giles Goat-Boy*, the reader, after he peels off all the layers of the onion, finds in the last layer only the impetus of story-telling.

As he constructs a much less intricate system of boxes in "Life-Story," Barth gives a clue about his purpose in using this technique. The boxes here contain imaginary authors. One of them, "D[,] is writing a fictional account of this conviction [that he is fictional, so] he has indisputably a fictional existence in his account. . . . E, hero of D's account, is said to be writing a similar account, and so the replication is in both ontological directions" (pp. 113–114). Barth also attacks on ontological grounds, because he denies the existence of the "real" world by showing that it is composed of layers related to each other in a way that makes them inseparable from imaginative constructs.

In "Dunyazadiad," the first novella in *Chimera*, Barth bases his system of boxes on the frame story of *The Thousand and One Nights*. That is, he tries to build a series of seven because an ifrit locked up his girl with seven padlocks. The genie, who represents Barth, admits that "he hoped one day to add to, and conceive a series of say, *seven* concentric stories-within-stories, so arranged that the climax of the innermost would precipitate that of the next tale out, and that of the next, et cetera" (p. 24). He does make seven layers inside the layer of himself: "The Dunyazadiad," Dunyazade's conversation with Shah Zaman, the story of Dunyazade and Scheherazade, the story of the genie, the stories that the genie tells to the girls (which are *The Thousand and One Nights*), the stories that Scheherazade tells to the King (the same stories) and Shah Zaman's story, told to Dunyazade. By the time the last layer appears, the stories from *The Thousand and One Nights* have been used up; that is, the main story, which has moved more quickly through time, has caught up with the frame story. Barth signals this by shifting to third person and by, at the very end, commenting on the whole process. Because of Barth's veiled appearance and of the Shah's retelling of the frame story of *The Thousand and One Nights*, this last layer does "precipitate that of the next tale out," causing the story line to move in the other direction through the layers. That is, it finishes the stories in previous layers, including

"Dunyazadiad," and it reintroduces the genie, this time without his disguise in a form even closer to Barth.

Despite the greater simplicity of the system in "Perseid," the second novella in *Chimera*, Barth makes an interesting point by relating in a curious way two of the levels. He makes the following layers inside the layer of himself: "Perseid," the story Perseus tells to Medusa (after they both have turned into constellations), the story Perseus tells to Calyxa, the story portrayed in the murals, the deeds of Perseus. Again the main story catches the frame story; Perseus leaves at II F 2 to perform further deeds, which the murals have not recorded. The strange relation occurs between the layers that contain the story Perseus tells Calyxa and the murals. Because she has drawn the murals, she already knows the story, at least in broad outline. These two levels intermingle, as in: "Calyxa insisted, and turned away, pouting as it were with her very scapulae, her back's small small, pouting I declare with her lean buttocks. 'No need to go on about small smalls and lean little buttocks' " (p. 95). Because she knows his thoughts, at this point the layer she creates, the murals, should come before the layer of his story. Also, the murals' aesthetic qualities may cause this phenomenon. "Intermingling" describes this relation less suitably than does "spirals back." That is, the layers spiral back, just like many other things in this story, and thus become "emblematic" as Barth told Israel Shenker he wished all the elements of his works to be.

This emblematic function needs clarification. It appears also in "Dunyazadiad," because the seven concentric circles that comprise the levels of reality in this novella, and comprise the novella itself, echo the seven padlocked boxes in which the ifrit places the girl. Similarly, the spiral effect of the layers in "Perseid" echos the spiraled murals, bedspread, Calyxa's navel, Calyxa's final existence as a spiral nebula, the motive of the novella (Barth's examination of, spiraling back over, his career) and the novella's plot (Perseus' ironic repetition of his earlier deeds). In other words, by creating these two works in geometric forms Barth has pushed one step further the Chinese box strategy, recapitulating these works in these figures and making everything in the work emblematic of everything else. Especially, form becomes meaning, and the work because it does not depend for meaning on the "real" world becomes as near to self-enclosed as it can get.

Spirals also control "Bellerophoniad," the third novella in *Chimera*, so again Barth makes the layers spiral. He creates five of them inside his own layer, to fit all the other fives in the novella: "Bellerophoniad," the story Bellerophon tells to Melanippe, the story Bellerophon tells to Philonoë and a layer made up of several parts, like the last layer of "Tlön, Uqbar, Orbis Tertius." This layer begins the spiraling back. It contains the information that Polyeidus wrote *Chimera*, which refers back to the outermost layer. The description of Bellerophon's meeting with Melanippe's mother refers back to the second layer. The quotation of Robert Graves's account of Bellerophon refers back to the fourth layer and also causes the main story line to catch, and begin to pass, the frame because Graves tells more of the story than the part that has happened up to this point of "Bellerophoniad." The letters from Polyeides, by equating him with Barth, and Bellerophon's lecture, which contains allusions to Barth, both refer to the layer of the author. Thus, at least one thing in this innermost layer connects with every other layer in the sequence. The last words of this novella, "it's no *Bellerophoniad*. It's a," spiral all the way out of this work to include the whole book (p. 308). "Chimera" will complete this last sentence, "chimera" in the sense that this word has acquired and, as it names the novel, the three-part entity (like the mythic animal) that Barth at this point of the book has just finished creating. The cross references throughout the book to the other novellas reinforce this point. The spiral continues back over Barth's early work. In *The Sot-Weed Factor* he unconsciously uses the conventions of the mythic hero. In *Giles Goat-Boy* he uses them consciously, and in *Chimera* he uses them consciously to comment on his earlier books.

Barth makes more elaborate Chinese boxes than the ones in Nabokov's and Borges's works. He knows the ontological implica-

tions of this device and he uses it to get immediately at these implications, and he develops this technique in an orderly way. In *The
Sot-Weed Factor* his use of Chinese boxes typifies the first stage of
the Literature of Exhaustion, because it creates and exhausts an infinite set of possibilities. In *Giles Goat-Boy, Lost in the Funhouse,*
and *Chimera*, however, he is less sanguine about literature and he
purports to fear that it has been exhausted already. Therefore, he
begins to use this hypothetical fear as his basic premise and to show
that all one needs in order to write fiction is a narrative impulse.

Barth also adds his own distinctive twist to the technique of the
Literature of Exhaustion that resembles the Chinese boxes, the
regressus in infinitum. First, he has combined it with the box technique in "Life-Story," since he uses the imaginary authors in this
story in both ways. He sometimes makes the elements of the infinite
series literary. Gerhard Joseph has noticed this same variation of
the technique in *Sot-Weed Factor*, and he identifies Barth's ante-
cedents: "Eben's defense of his virginity which echoes that of
Joseph Andrews which in turn parodies that of Pamela, etc., creates
the *regressus in infinitum* effect that Barth admires in the fictions
of Nabokov and Borges, the literary funhouse in which the reader
is invited to amuse himself."[2] If this technique operating in the
imaginary world can keep alive the spark of narrative, operating
in the real world it can show that the contents of that world have
no reality after all. Eierkopf, a mad scientist in *Giles Goat-Boy,*
uses this technique to separate tick and tock, which he considers,
wrongly, to be absolutes and opposites. He works on the knife-edge
of a clock, trying to "halve and halve again, *ad infinitum*, the width
of the edge, until theoretically it reached a perfect point at the
center of the hole and the midpoint of the Tick-Tock swing" (p.
482). He insanely conceives this project, as one would expect from
a character whose name is German for "egghead." The infinite regress strategy multiplies possibilities, and although this gains an
advantage for an author trying to keep alive a moribund genre, it
presents an insurmountable disadvantage for a person trying to
control variables in the real world in order to accomplish something.

It follows that, to be dealt with successfully, the real world must be circumscribed and thus become less rich than the world of the imagination.

Barth attacks the same kinds of literature that Borges and Nabokov have badly scarred, the various kinds of realistic fiction. The novel differentiated itself from other kinds of prose fiction and attained its status as an independent genre because of its realism, so an anti-realist must dispel the belief that novels must perforce be realistic. Barth tries to do this by showing that realism had to be invented, too, that it was not just *there* to be accepted as the natural mode for writers to use. He describes in "Anonymiad" a bard inventing a new kind of literature, and claims that "the whole conception of a literature faithful to daily reality is among the innovations of this novel opus" (p. 176). He attacks another disturbing bias in favor of realism by claiming that this mode of literature does not avoid artifice but merely uses another kind of artifice. Among the intercalated comments on the art of fiction in "Lost in the Funhouse" is this one: "Initials, blanks, or both were often substituted for proper names in nineteenth-century fiction to enhance the illusion of reality. . . . Interestingly, as with other aspects of realism, it is an *illusion* that is being enhanced, by purely artificial means" (pp. 69–70).

If a reader becomes convinced that realism should not be the criterion by which he can measure modes of literature but only one among many modes, he can calculate its strengths and weaknesses. The problems of opposites and of unity and duality continually foil realists, as Barth shows in the plot of many of his works by having the characters who accept a realistic world view try to deal with opposites. Besides George, Eben Cooke in *The Sot-Weed Factor* and the Siamese twin in "Petition" cannot cope with this matter. The twin presents the more graphic example, since he has to deal with opposites not only philosophically but also physically. Barth makes sure that these characters try in various ways to make sense of and deal with the world by conceiving of it as a system of opposites. When all of these ways fail, Barth expects the reader to conclude that dividing the world into opposites does not make sense. Opposition, like space and time, is one of the basic constituents of the commonsense notion of the world, so if realism cannot deal with it, realism's claim to superiority among literary modes loses its credibility. Because it cannot make sense of opposites, realism cannot do what it claims, accurately mimic the world. Barth's paradigmatic realist is the nymph for whom "Echo" is named. She seems to imitate exactly but she always distorts slightly, usually by omission. A reader who can agree with Barth up to this point will probably concede the next point in his chain of reasoning, that as long as all modes of literature, including realism, are artificial instead of mimetic, writers might just as well revel in their artifice.

The realists have problems not only because of the distortion of the lens they turn on the world, but also because of the world's distortions. The latter does not correct the lens's distortions; it compounds them. As Barth becomes more determined about his anti-realism his characters become more convinced of the world's absurdity. In *The Floating Opera* and *The End of the Road* his characters consider that they may be living in a chaotic world. Burlingame in *The Sot-Weed Factor* speaks the most fervently for this position. He says of man, "he is by mindless lust engendered and by mindless wrench expelled, from the Eden of the womb to the motley, mindless world. He is Chance's fool, the toy of aimless Nature—a mayfly flitting down the winds of Chaos" (p. 364). Nothing in this novel except Barth's art contradicts Burlingame's statement, but that exception is absolutely crucial.

Better worlds exist in the imagination, so writers should turn their backs on the lunacy of mundane existence and devise their own sane and orderly worlds. Barth has admitted that he wishes to devise his own worlds: the "impulse to imagine alternatives to the world can become a driving impulse for writers. I confess that it is for me."[3] He dramatizes this impulse in *Giles Goat-Boy*, the novel he was writing when he made this statement. In a "cover letter" J. B., an obvious mask for Barth, describes his meeting with the strange creature who brought him the manuscript that forms the body of this novel. The emphasis in this scene falls on J. B.'s visitor and his book, but J. B. himself is important, too, because he is a writer. Using Wittgenstein's terms, he talks about the book he is writing: "My hero, I explained, was to be a Cosmic Amateur; a man enchanted with history, geography, nature, the people around him —everything that *is the case*—because he saw its arbitrariness but couldn't understand or accept its finality" (p. xxvii). This accurately describes the agony that afflicts the characters in Barth's first three books. More important, it describes Barth's attitude toward his material in those books. In this illuminating speech he abjures his former belief that order can be found in the world, finally understanding and accepting the absurdity of the world and vowing to write about what he will establish as the case. One warning is necessary here. It is a serious error to call Barth an Existentialist because of his vision of chaos. His pointing out of absurdity is only one, and a minor one at that, of his ways to attack reality. Furthermore, his attack on reality matters less than does the edifice he erects where reality once stood.

Like Borges and Nabokov, but less consistently, Barth denies the validity of autobiographical fiction, and he less successfully eliminates traces of autobiography from his works. The events of his life sometimes make their way into his work—for instance, in the descriptions of Todd Andrews's years at Johns Hopkins in *Floating Opera* and in the academic writer J. B.—though of course neither description is perfectly autobiographical. A story in *Lost in the Funhouse*, although based on his life, is far from accurate autobiography. In "Ambrose His Mark" he turns the life of his own German-American family into the fictional equivalent of a Katzenjammer Kids cartoon. These uses of autobiography are all incidental, however. More interesting and less autobiographical in the strict sense, his recreation of the Eastern Shore of Maryland describes the area where he grew up. He writes about it in an essay called "Land-scape: The Eastern Shore."[4] This region provides the backdrop for *Floating Opera, End of the Road, The Sot-Weed Factor* and some of the stories in *Lost in the Funhouse. Chimera* contains quite a few references to Barth, both to his literary career and his relations with women. Autobiography serves him mainly as material on which his memory can work to create an ambiance for his fiction. In other words, he uses his life much as Borges uses his, mainly as the source of a setting.

This psychological dimension of his life contributes little to his work. One of his characters, a writer, confesses that in both his art and his life the same things interest him. But he qualifies this confession drastically: "among their other, more serious preoccupations" (*Funhouse*, p. 121). This description, with the qualification, applies also to Barth's use of autobiography. Barth considers most important the aesthetic themes that lie at the heart of his work and the aesthetic methods that he has developed to turn material, whether autobiographical or not, into art. He understands that he cannot describe his life any more accurately than he can describe the rest of reality. The story which, oddly comprises the narrative voice of "Autobiography" agrees that it, and presumably all fiction, distorts its author (p. 34). An author faced with the impossibility of creating accurate autobiography in fiction should admit from the beginning that supposedly autobiographical material in fiction merely comprises part of the artifice. This admission certainly clarifies one of Barth's stories. In "Echo" Narcissus' self-absorption makes him the figure of the autobiographical artist. But appearances are deceiving: "Narcissus would appear to be opposite from Echo: he perishes by denying all except himself; she persists by effacing herself absolutely. Yet they come to the same: it was never himself Narcissus craved, but his reflection, the Echo of his fancy . . . the voice persists" (p. 99). The Echo (the story) and the voice (the artistic means that produced it), and not the autobiographical elements in the story, are the more serious preoccupations that Barth points to here.

In summary, things in fiction that seem to be part of the real world because of their similarity to things one knows about the author actually belong to a fictive world. That is, despite their previous status they become unreal when they appear in the world of art. Furthermore, Barth daringly implies that these same auto-biographical facts, like everything else that appears to be part of someone's life, have no inherent reality. The narrator of "Life-Story" makes this unnerving claim. Barth's use of autobiography thus leads to a suggestion that at best life is no more real than art, and perhaps it is not real at all.

Barth has avoided social and political concerns with even more determination than he has avoided autobiography. The surprise caused by his rare comments on these matters makes them more effective. A good example can be found in each of his two long books, but others are scarce. He claims in *The Sot-Weed Factor* that Eben Cooke "belonged . . . to the class of the exploiters; as an educated gentleman of the western world he had shared in the fruits of his culture's power and must therefore share what guilt that power incurred" (p. 579). In *Giles Goat-Boy* he more scathingly lists Peter Greene's middle-American qualities: "open-handedness, vulgarity, fair dealing, bad manners, good intentions, gullibility, straight-forwardness, lack of culture, abundance of wealth, and sen-timentality" (p. 285). Except for those rare instances, Barth has conformed to his stated lack of interest in social criticism. In an essay, "Muse, Spare Me," he asks to be spared from "Social-Historical Responsibility."⁵ In his *Wisconsin Studies* interview he makes a similar announcement of his unconcern about these matters (p. 13).

He also assiduously avoids conventional history because of its connection with time and "reality." Like the rest of "reality," however, it is not real at all. Just as *Pale Fire* makes its readers skeptical of literary criticism, *The Sot-Weed Factor* makes its readers doubt the history that they probably have so blithely ac-cepted. The obviously spurious journals in this novel start one wondering whether he should trust all the other journals that have been used as historical evidence. Barth does not always attack his-tory as mildly as he does here. Once he works more subtly and unobtrusively. In *The Sot-Weed Factor* he produces an effect like the layers of Troy, with the newer obscuring the older. He wrote this novel during the twentieth century, but from the present it goes back to the eighteenth century for its technique, then further back to the late seventeenth century for its main action and finally back to the early seventeenth century for the action described in the journals of John Smith and Henry Burlingame I, for which the main characters search throughout most of the book. Once a reader sees these three overlays covering the "events" described in the journals, he cannot deny his inability to understand history directly. That is, people cannot conceive directly of history; it is a construct, just like literature.

After novelists dispel the aura of certainty that surrounds history, they can use it. In "Muse, Spare Me," Barth clearly delineates the uses to which he puts history: "the use of historical or legendary material, especially in a farcical spirit, has a number of technical virtues, among which are esthetic distance and the opportunity for counter-realism" (pp. 443–444). Thus, he manages to subordinate history to his own aesthetic ends, whereas realists subordinate their art to historical probability, if not to something they consider to be historical actuality. Barth treats history in a mildly farcical way in *Giles Goat-Boy* because he incongruously mixes historical allegory with other allegories. He produces his most clever historical farce in *The Sot-Weed Factor*, by sexualizing history. He invents a homosexual dimension for both Isaac Newton and Henry More and a lusty heterosexual one for John Smith, and he "argues" that these dimensions determined their roles in history.

In order to simplify the complexities of Barth's psychology one should consider his first two novels in addition to the others. *Floating Opera* and *End of the Road* have fairly realistic decorums, so a reader has the right to expect fairly accurate and profound psychology in them. Gerhard Joseph argues that these novels do not contain that kind of psychology because Barth has sacrificed it to his intellectual schemes, particularly in the latter novel (p. 20). This matter probably cannot be settled to everyone's satisfaction since the intellectual schemes form part of the decorum and since it is difficult to decide whether realism or these schemes should give way when they conflict. In other words, Joseph's first point, that some of the characters' motivations do not make sense realistically, is true, but it is an open issue whether this is a flaw.

Barth uses a different kind of psychology in his obviously non-realistic works like *Giles Goat-Boy*. In this novel Barth draws characters that Robert Scholes likens to prenovelistic ones.[6] Because *Giles Goat-Boy* is, among other things, a novel of ideas, one looks for the interesting psychology in the ideas of the characters. Scholes also clarifies this dimension of the novel, pointing out that Kennard Sear is a debased Freudian, and Max Spielman a Jungian. Barth treats Sear with the same contempt that Nabokov pours onto his Freudians, but he treats Max more sympathetically. Barth's handling of this aspect of Sear and Spielman, however, relates to psychological theory, not to psychology per se, and it provides more material for Barth to put to his own uses.

In *Giles Goat-Boy* Barth allegorically treats social, political, historical and psychological matters. Scholes has worked out in great detail the meanings of these allegories, so there is no need to do it again. However, I sound a warning about deducing from all this material that this novel is basically realistic. As I mentioned, Barth eventually discredits the allegories by discrediting the absolutes on which they depend. That is, Barth uses material congenial to realists but he does so in his own way and for his own nonrealistic purposes.

One of his major purposes is to write literature that openly displays its artificiality. He sees no reason to apologize about being nonrealistic. In his *Wisconsin Studies* interview he says, "a different way to come to terms with the discrepancy between art and the Real Thing is to *affirm* the artificial element in art (you can't get rid of it anyhow), and make the artifice part of your point" (p. 6). This strategy can lead to a deadening preciosity. Jack Richardson opens his review of *Lost in the Funhouse* with a list of the flaws that emphasizing artifice can cause, but then claims that Barth's talents have minimized these flaws almost to the point of nonexistence.[7] Barth himself knows about the dangers of this method. In "Life-Story" an imaginary author complains about his own work: "Who doesn't prefer art that at least overtly imitates something other than its own processes? That doesn't continually proclaim 'Don't forget I'm artifice!' " (p. 114). Besides talent, which for Richardson justifies this kind of literature, making clear one's purpose in displaying artifice can also allay readers' suspicions about the value of obviously artificial literature. Barth certainly makes clear enough his purpose: to attack realism.

Robert Scholes explains the most striking announcement of artifice in Barth's work (p. 169). This is the passage in *Giles Goat-Boy* in which the hero comes upon a girl who reveals that she is reading *Giles Goat-Boy* and has got to the precise place in the book where she is described reading (p. 725). Elsewhere he announces his artifice more conventionally. The apparatus at its beginning and ending also emphasize this novel's artificiality. He includes a publisher's disclaimer and a cover-letter to the editors and publishers at the beginning, and a posttape, a postscript to the posttape and a footnote to the postscript to the posttape at the end. In *Lost in the Funhouse* Barth comments on narrative technique as he tells the title story. His idiosyncratic styles also call attention to themselves and away from his subject matter. He uses this last technique most notably in the imitation eighteenth century syle of *The Sot-Weed Factor*, but his style always has a Protean quality, changing magically to suit his purpose.

Barth uses fewer allusions than Borges and Nabokov, and unlike them he alludes more often to history than to literature. However, though he uses other means more often to give his work its literary quality, allusions do play some role in his fiction. Besides its mythological references, *Lost in the Funhouse* contains passing references to other writers. The first story, "Night-Sea Journey," has many literary allusions; one of the most surprising refers to Tertullian—"I can believe them *because* they are absurd"—and a more easily recognized one refers to Ginsberg: "I have seen the best swimmers of my generation go under" (p. 3, p. 4). In his interview he expresses admiration for two authors, who, it turns out, have given him ideas. Machado de Assis is interested in twins (e.g., Esau and Jacob), an important subject in *The Sot-Weed Factor*. Robert Musil may have inspired Barth's interest in nihilism, triangles, and attacking history as no more than a story; these themes appear prominently in *The Man Without Qualities*.

The Sot-Weed Factor contains Barth's most interesting allusions. The list of Eben's favorite books, early in the novel, provides useful clues to the rest of that novel. Heroic tales like the *Odyssey*, the *Book of Martyrs* and the *Lives of the Saints* contrast with this account of a comic hero. Ovid's *Metamorphoses* provides some inspiration for the characterization of Burlingame. The mode of *The Sot-Weed Factor* resembles that of the romances that Eben likes. His two books on virgins have shaped his attitudes toward sex. Besides Eben's books, the eighteenth century novel of course greatly influences *The Sot-Weed Factor*. Barth has written an afterword to the Signet edition of *Roderick Random*, and his own novel, like Smollet's, is picaresque, has a ubiquitous servant and ends on the familial estate. Besides its characteristic style, Barth borrows many themes from this era of the novel: disguise, reality and appearance, incest, coincidence, paternity, etc. Fielding's preface to *Joseph Andrews* clarifies not only his contemporaries' work but also Barth's. His definition of the comic romance—"a comic epic in prose"—fits *The Sot-Weed Factor*, and the domain he claims for himself—the ridiculous, which arises from either vanity or hypocrisy—is also Barth's.

Barth's most interesting use of other literature occurs in *Chimera*, where he frequently mentions his own work. He wrote this book at the probable midpoint of his career, which encouraged him to find out where he was and where he was going by finding out where he had been. He conceived this book as a spiral back over his career. As he gets into the book he begins to refer to the other novellas in it as well and to make the novel a metaphor of his writer's block. He also puts himself into the book, in the thinly disguised figures of the genie in "Dunyazadiad" and Polyeidus in "Bellerophoniad" and in the only slightly more carefully disguised characters who try simultaneously to solve their narrative and sexual problems. These disguises allow him to write about his own work.

Barth's references to other works matter less than his use of literary history and theory in his fiction. He has been interested in aesthetic themes since the beginning of his career, and they form one of the connections between his first two books and the others. In order to understand fully the theme of art in *The Floating Opera* one must separate Todd Andrews from Barth. The former is the nihilist and absurdist; the latter has an answer, art, to man's plight. Barth dramatically juxtaposes the order of art and the absurdity of life in the climactic scene on the showboat. While Todd prepares for suicide, an actor recites Hamlet's soliloquy on suicide to a demonstratively unappreciative audience. Todd, as always, does not realize that the alternative of art is valid even when its manifestation is quite pathetic, and his reasons for avoiding suicide have nothing to do with a new commitment to aesthetic matters.

In *The Floating Opera* Barth's development of the alternative of art begins with an image, the boat. The captain expounds at length on the care and skill of its builders. The implication, which Todd does not draw, is that any well made object justifies itself. This holds even for a gaudy showboat that carries vulgar entertainment. Since the boat also represents life, which Barth explicitly makes clear, this point holds for life, too: it may be otherwise absurd, but craftsmanship can make it meaningful. Specifically, the act of writing, if well done, can be meaningful even if the artist has only absurd materials to work with. From his conversation with the captain Todd should have drawn the self-satisfying conclusion that his Inquiry justifies his existence. Paradoxically, it does so while it fails to explain that existence to him. In other words, content matters little; man should concern himself with creating pleasing forms, particularly artistic forms.

The narrator's or author's adroit shaping of his material suffices. Barth emphasizes this shaping by creating a garrulous narrator. Todd frequently breaks the illusion by pointing out that he is narrating a story. He comments on the difficulty of telling a story, warns against interpreting some symbols but explains others and generally calls attention to himself. After a while the reader understands that the personal part of the Inquiry, which Todd occasionally mentions as it piles up beside him in peach baskets, has become this novel. Despite all his self-consciousness, Todd never realizes that his role as author by itself makes his life meaningful.

The same contrast between world and art appears in *End of the Road*. The chaotic world of this novel contains a man who flaunts his rationality but cannot understand his life, another who periodically becomes immobile, a zany therapist, and exotic situations. Barth contrasts this madness with an ideal world of art, in which everything is sensible and ordered. Music provides an alternative to chaotic life, and Jake Horner can escape it by dancing or listening to records of graceful Mozart compositions. A statue of Laocoön is the most frequently mentioned work of art. Jake thinks that it changes its form in order to mimic him or another character or to comment on the action. Sometimes it symbolizes man's restrictions. At the end of the novel Jake leaves this statue behind, because he has been unable to learn its secret: that it, coherent and meaningful, like all art, can provide answers to perplexed people.

Again Barth scatters hints throughout the novel so the reader can see what the main character misses. As a teacher of grammar Jake constantly examines language, the link he needs, because the kind of art that could save him is literature. He recognizes this possibility, but only theoretically, when he sees that inadequacies in language lead to anguish. Rennie Morgan goes through psychological torment because she feels both love and hate for her husband but has no word to represent her feeling so that she can understand it. Dogmatic Joe tries to fit reality to a philosophical system; Jake sees the futility of this but then gives up trying to create order. The best alternative, this novel suggests, is fitting language into meaningful patterns, that is, making literature. In his book, too, the narrative voice calls attention to itself, as if to say above the din of the confused characters that it has the answer.

Barth's virtuoso performance in *The Sot-Weed Factor*, an eighteenth-century novel written in the twentieth century, makes this novel, more clearly than the first two, a work of literature about literature. Less obviously, in it Barth recapitulates most of the main features of American literature. Richard Noland lists the features that Barth incorporates: "the idea of innocence, the place of the artist in American society, the Indian as evil or noble savage, the wilderness as paradise or anti-paradise, the initiation into society, the problem of identity, and the international theme."[8] Also, the improbabilities, sometimes even contradictions, of the plot and the infinite possibilities offered by the strategy of inventing journals suggest that this is a literary artifice completely controlled by the author. To use Barth's term from his afterword to *Roderick Random*, the "adventurousness" that dominates the plot suggests something that Eben knows: "that lives are stories, he assumed; that stories end, he allowed—how else could one begin another? But that the story teller himself must live a particular tale and die—Unthinkable!" (p. 288).

In *Giles Goat-Boy* Barth more ambitiously handles the theme of art, for he presents a capsule history of literature. As a basis for this history Barth amplifies one of his favorite theories. He hypothesizes that ontogeny recapitulates not only phylogeny but also cosmogeny. He attributes this addition to the familiar theory to Max Spielman, one of his characters (p. 43, 300). The ontogeny is George's growth; the phylogeny is the development of mankind into heroes; the cosmogeny, reflecting Barth's belief that literature forms the basic stuff of reality, is the history of literature. Throughout most of the book Barth uses ancient Greek genres, linguistically justifying his combination of them by making his hero part goat. He implies this justification in *Lost in the Funhouse*, where he mentions that both tragedy and satire derive from goats (pp. 190–191). The Dionysian origin of tragedy supports his point about tragedy, though his etymology is questionable in regard to satire (he prefers fruitful ideas to proper etymology). He makes the satire in *Giles Goat-Boy* clear enough, and the similarities between George and

Oedipus, as well as Barth's revised version of *Oedipus the King*, supply the tragedy. Goats also relate to pastoral literature, the dominant mode at the beginning of the book. And because pastoral literature and comedy had the same muse, Thalia, to whom Barth occasionally refers in *Lost in the Funhouse*, he can logically use comedy, too, in this book, and of course he does. *Giles Goat-Boy* also has elements of another ancient genre, the epic, though this genre has no ostensible connection with goats. In his *Wisconsin Studies* interview Barth calls this novel a comic Old Testament, which seems true, and also is consistent with his linguistic reason for mixing genres because of all the sheep and goat imagery in the Bible. The final connection between goats and ancient forms of literature is that early works were often written on vellum: goat skin.

As this novel progresses so do the ontogeny and cosmogeny. In the last part of *Giles Goat-Boy* the hero becomes less goatish and more human. Meanwhile literature has progressed until it reaches the modern genres, which do not relate to goats. Two genres alternate in this part of the book. After it becomes clear that George is not a hero, which makes epic themes inappropriate, the book often reads like a fairly conventional novel, even at times a love story. At this point it also has examples of the Literature of Exhaustion clearly visible on the surface instead of hidden below it, like the involuted scene that describes the girl who is reading *Giles Goat-Boy*. *Giles Goat-Boy* deals at least as much with literature as it does with George, this novel's hero.

Lost in the Funhouse is even more basically about literature. On a superficial level, it contains many statements about narrative technique and sometimes discusses the state of fiction from the perspective of the Literature of Exhaustion. In "Title" Barth says that the novel has four possibilities now: rejuvenation, development of new genres, using the impossibility of creating something new as the basis of something new, and silence (pp. 105–106). More importantly, the organizing principle of this collection of short fictions makes a point about literature. Barth claims in the "Author's Note" that he has carefully organized this book, but it takes some searching to find his principle. It turns out to be the same hypothesis that he uses in *Giles Goat-Boy*, that ontogeny recapitulates phylogeny and cosmogeny. He introduces the three developments in the first story, "Night-Sea Journey." The ontogeny is the development of the sperm that narrates the story and of Ambrose, the hero of some of the fictions. The phylogeny is the growth of the human race until it can produce a hero; at first, a conventional hero like those who embark on mythic night sea journeys, and later, artist-heroes. The aspects of the book, like the awakening to sex and language and the vocation scenes, that are modelled on the *Künstlerroman* tradition describe this last development. These last features also form part of the cosmogeny, which is again literary.

In *Lost in the Funhouse* Barth foreshortens the early development of literature in order to trace the development further and describe more fully the Literature of Exhaustion. In the early stories he considers whether literature is possible and if so, whether he can justify spending time creating it. "Ambrose His Mark" deals with an essential question, one that needs an affirmative answer before literature can even begin: whether language, and thus literature, can accommodate itself to reality. A family tries hard to name a child and finally decides on "Ambrose" when bees cover him. Their decision suggests that language needs a cultural background; if it did not the child could have been named "bee" instead of being named after a saint associated with bees. Barth mentions many historical and legendary characters in whose lives bees played an important part, but he omits the story that is the paradigm of his book. According to mythology, Aristaeus, trying to find out what angered his bees, learns the story of Orpheus and Eurydice. This story of the archetypal artist and foiled lover is the controlling myth of *Lost in the Funhouse*.

"Autobiography" and "Water-Message" also examine the possibility and validity of literature. A story narrates the former, discussing its birth and its parents: an author and a tape recorder. The narrative voice claims that language can become literature, because the author speaking into a tape recorder has created this story. The latter fiction ends by dramatizing the fact that reality can be transformed into language. A young boy finds a piece of paper with words written on it and, more surprisingly, with a bit of wood pulp visible in it. He then remembers that pulp is physically transformed into paper; symbolically this indicates that reality can become language and literature.

The next section of the book considers realism, especially its weaknesses. "Petition" deals with the familiar problems of duality and unity and the relation of opposites, stumbling blocks for rationality and realism. When he describes the distorting mirrors of the funhouse in "Lost in the Funhouse" Barth scoffs at realism's claim that it can mirror reality. He suggests a typical alternative to realism when he affirms that mirrors distort and when he uses the funhouse as a symbol of art, which must be nonrealistic.

By the next section of the book literature begins to show signs of exhaustion, and Barth begins to seek remedies. The title character of "Echo" must repeat the words of others, just as a novelist late in the history of his genre feels that he can only repeat his predecessors. This story also marks the beginning of Barth's reliance on a strategy that he can use to combat exhaustion: retelling myths. In "Two Meditations" he repeats situations: in the first one the straw that broke the camel's back, in the second the belief that pollution leads to knowledge. In "Title" he lays out the four possibilities for literature. This story expresses his doubts about nonrealistic writing: "weld iron rods into abstract patterns, say, and you've still got real iron, but arrange words into abstract patterns and you've got nonsense" (p. 109). In "Glossolalia" he returns to the technique of repetitions, this time repeating styles.

By the final section of the book authors have developed the Literature of Exhaustion and other postrealistic literature. "Life-Story" clearly belongs to the Literature of Exhaustion: involuted, containing Chinese boxes, arguing that life is a fiction. But it also shows some skepticism about this kind of literature, because it charges that

turning completely away from the everyday world indicates schizophrenia (p. 115). "Menelaiad" takes this kind of literature about as
far as possible, perhaps to the point of self-parody, for it has a very
large number of Chinese boxes. In the final story, "Anonymiad,"
Barth makes a fresh start. He tells the story of a man who creates
the novel out of the materials of the epic and invents writing. That
is, this imaginary author has successfully dealt with a situation
of ultimacy.

Some of Barth's uses of myth should by now be clear, like the
function of the Orpheus myth in "Ambrose His Mark" and the
retelling of myths in other stories in *Lost in the Funhouse*. Also
obviously, he depends on the stories of heroes. He claims in his
interview that the similarity between Eben and Burlingame, on one
hand, and the archetypal hero as described by Lord Raglan, on the
other, is accidental, but that he read Raglan's *The Hero* before he
wrote *Giles Goat-Boy*, in which he tried to make his hero fulfill all
the requirements set down by Raglan. However, one matter relating
to myth in his work does need clarification. The mytho-therapy
mentioned in *End of the Road* has a misleading name, for it involves
not myth-making but arbitrary choosing and then asserting those
choices. In other words, it is the same attitude that Burlingame
advocates and Eben spurns, except in an opium dream (p. 365; p.
480).

Thus, Barth has the same interests in subject matter as Borges
and Nabokov. However, his work turns back upon itself more often
than theirs does. They seem to have followed their inclinations,
whereas he seems to have a keener sense of the state of literature
and a stronger feeling that he belongs to a literary advance guard.
He does not necessarily have more insight; he has had the advantage
of coming to maturity as a writer later than Borges and Nabokov,
after more experimental writing has been done. In any case, he
neatly recapitulates his work in the Moebius strip he has had
printed at the beginning of *Lost in the Funhouse* along with in-
structions for cutting it out and assembling it. Because the strip

is self-enclosed, an infinite number of trips around it is possible, and because of the words printed on it, following the strip and reading the words produces an infinite, self-enclosed story.

Because of his premise that the novel is dying, in his fiction he directs much of the attention to problems of various genres. A writer can comically expose the idiosyncracies of genres by parodying them, a technique he uses especially in *Giles Goat-Boy*. His parody of *Oedipus the King* is the most extensive example, but he also parodies prayer and, like Nabokov, scholarship (p. 455; p. 452). And this novel as a whole parodies allegory. Gerhard Joseph accurately describes how Barth does this: "the primary way in which Barth parodies the traditional techniques of allegory is to jump with tonal and thematic abandon among the various referents of his allegory" (p. 34). In *The Sot-Weed Factor* he parodies the epic, as Russell Miller indicates.[9] Barth probably intended to base an entire book on parody when he made his cryptic remark in "The Literature of Exhaustion" that *The Sot-Weed Factor* and *Giles Goat-Boy* are "novels which imitate the form of the Novel, by an author who imitates the role of Author" (p. 33). Such parodic imitation underlines the artificiality of the book.

But if one believes that the novel is dying, parody becomes merely a holding action. One can really nullify death by inventing a new form. First he must mix old forms, hoping that the result will be viable and coherent enough to claim the status of a new genre. The narrator of "Anonymiad" does this, for by putting epic materials in prose form he produces a genre that he calls fiction, although that label seems peculiar to modern readers. Besides the history, fiction and myth of the hero that clearly appear in *The Sot-Weed Factor*, this book has a few less obvious genres. Its characterization, plot and emphasis on idea qualify it for inclusion in the category of anatomies that Northrop Frye has created. Often lost in the welter of genres in *The Sot-Weed Factor* is a basic one: it comments on a poem, like a book that differs vastly from it, *Pale Fire*. In *Giles Goat-Boy*, too, Barth has mixed genres. Joseph calls it "a hybrid of genres: part sacred book, animal fable, science-fiction fantasy, political allegory, educational satire, epic, and what not else" (p. 32).

Barth has also taken the next step and actually invented a new form of literature, which one day may become an independent genre. Taking his cue from the technological world around him, in *Lost in the Funhouse* he has written pieces intended to be read aloud with part of the narration coming through a tape recorder. Michel Butor's *Niagra* (1965), a novel in the form of a radio play, is perhaps the nearest thing to a predecessor of Barth's book. In public readings from this book he has used tape recorders and shown that his apparently jocular explanation, in the "Author's Note," of the media he intended for each work in *Funhouse* should be taken seriously. This explanation ends with a comment on "Title" that shows the scope of his experiments with tape recorded literature: " 'Title' makes somewhat separate but equally valid senses in several media: print, monophonic recorded authorial voice, stereophonic ditto in dialogue with itself, live authorial voice, live ditto in dialogue with monophonic ditto aforementioned, and live ditto interlocutory with stereophonic et cetera, my own preference; it's been 'done' in all six" (p. ix). In short, he has played the bard, not with a lyre but with a tape recorder. He has not created mere stunts, despite the tongue-in-cheek quality of his list of possibilities for "Title," but effective works that mean more with the tape recorder than they do in print.

Borges, Nabokov, and Barth handle in the same ways their most common themes and take nearly the same attitudes toward these themes. Like the other two writers, Barth abhors time, although he uses this theme less often than they do. He even shares with them an interest in the paradox of Achilles, whom he calls Peleides in *Giles Goat-Boy*, and the tortoise. He also, like the other two writers, reports the destruction of his time-obsessed characters. Eierkopf, the mad scientist in *Giles Goat-Boy* who tries to separate tick from tock, is battered almost to death by the apparatus of a giant clock, an appropriate punishment.

Fleeing the world of time, Barth tries to imagine a timeless, idyllic world. Eben in *The Sot-Weed Factor* believes that preservation of innocence will allow him to escape the clutches of time. In one of his poems he writes:

> Preserv'd, my Innocence preserveth Me
>   From Life, from Time, from Death, from History;
> Without it I must breathe Man's mortal Breath:
>   Commence a Life—and thus commence my Death!
>
> (p. 71)

His purpose amounts to preserving the bliss of his childhood, the same refuge from time that the Veens in *Ada* sought to retain, though certainly not with sexual innocence. Barth himself succeeds in fending off time, in the usual sense of creating art that will endure, but also in a more original sense. He has created art that seems timeless not only because it is art but also because it is a certain kind of art. As his career has progressed he has managed to create an ever stronger sense of timelessness. As Joseph mentions, Barth's "flight from realism to parodic fable turns out to be a flight from time to timelessness" (p. 7). Barth's device, in all three of the novellas in *Chimera*, of having the main action catch up to the frame story also disputes conventional notions of time. In "Perseid" he also scrambles the time sequence when Athene appears. Thus, in this book he shows the arbitrariness of fictional time sequences in order to suggest the arbitrariness of "real" time sequences. Joseph also implicitly points out the basis of the Literature of Exhaustion's attitude toward time: its equations of destructive time with realism, and of blissful timelessness with itself and other forms of non-realistic literature.

Barth treats rarely but negatively time's acolyte, memory. He associates it, too, with a realistic view of the world, which Eben Cooke defends. He tells Burlingame: "Thy *memory* served as thy credentials, did it not? 'Tis the house of Identity, the Soul's dwelling place: Thy memory, my memory, the memory of the race: 'tis the constant from which we measure change; the sun. Without it, all were Chaos right enough' " (p. 141). Eben's florid rhetoric bespeaks more conviction than his logic justifies. He reveals his mistake by his failure to recognize that all is indeed chaos. His naive dependence on memory and other tools of the realist causes disaster after disaster for him.

Some other examples of negative themes that appear in Barth's work as well as in Borges's and Nabokov's are the repetition of events in "Two Meditations," the repetition of style in "Glossolalia" and the fear expressed by the narrator of "Life-Story" that overly-patterned art is schizophrenic. The latter opinion contradicts the position of the other two writers, who approve of artistic patterns and disapprove of imposing patterns on life. Possibly Barth does not completely agree with the others on these issues, but the scarcity of his references to these themes suggests instead that he thinks that the enemies have been routed by Borges and Nabokov, who he claims as allies, so that he need not repeat the attacks but can concentrate on developing positive themes. In short, he recognizes his position in the second generation of the tradition in which he works, and he knows that this can be advantageous.

He agrees with the theory that the domains usually called real and imaginary can be reversed. Sometimes he tries to make this reversal through language, as Campbell Tatham points out. In regard to the scene that describes the "Beist in the buckwheat," Tatham says, "there is the lesser set of abstractions, the poetry reading which suggests that art can in some way replace reality. . . . While the boy who is persistently seducing the girl in the pasture . . . is able to keep straight the distinctions between poems and copulation, between art and reality, George confuses the two."[10] Barth embeds this suggestion so deeply in the texture of his work, particularly in *Giles Goat-Boy* and *Lost in the Funhouse*, that it takes this kind of close reading to pry it loose. Examples are numerous, and once a reader learns to look for this technique he can, with attention, discover them for himself.

In *Chimera* the literary realm almost eclipses the "real" realm. He starts slowly in "Dunyazadiad," having Scheherazade repeat "the key to the treasure is the treasure" simultaneously with the genie when she wants him to appear. Thus, language can control part of everyday reality. In "Perseid" this controlling force becomes art. The murals in his temple remind Perseus of the early part of his life so that he can tell it to Calyxa and so that he can ironically repeat it. At the end of the story Perseus becomes not only a constellation but also this story being transformed into a work of literature. Similarly, Bellerophon "turned into written words," into "a version of Bellerophon's life" (p. 138). That is, Bellerophon becomes "Bellerophoniad." Polyeidus, another character in this novella, also becomes this novella (p. 165). Bellerophon's killing of the Chimera with a pencil, an instrument of writing, combines with these other things to indicate that "the truth of fiction is that Fact is fantasy; the made-up story is a model of the world" (p. 246).

Unlike Borges, Barth does not frontally attack reality by claiming that it is a dream. He suggests, more moderately, that life is *like* a dream, an opium dream. Moreover, he makes this suggestion only by implication, in a description of an opium dream that Eben has. He dreams that he is climbing mountains and is faced with a difficult choice of routes, so he decides to make an arbitrary choice and see it through. He does not realize it but here he follows Burlingame's advice that one should admit the absurdity of life and assert himself through arbitrary choice. Aside from this brief passage Barth has little interest in dreams.

To him the world dissolves not into dreams but into language. His theory of the linguistic basis of reality has been related to some of the aspects of his work that have been discussed. The visibility of a bit of wood pulp in a piece of paper in "Water-Message" and the equally dramatic invention of writing in "Anonymiad" show readers how remarkable it is that men can transmute reality into literature. Also in the naming of Ambrose in "Ambrose His Mark" language must be fitted to reality, and this story, too, implies that this process is not automatic but difficult. The relation of this theme to so many others demonstrates its centrality to Barth's vision.

Barth has known for some time that trouble results if someone attaches the wrong word to an object or if he can find no word for an object. Early in his career, in *End of the Road,* he describes the trouble that develops from Rennie Morgan's lack of a word for the combination of love and hate. One of George's assignments in *Giles Goat-Boy* turns out to be purely a linguistic problem. He has failed to fix the clock because he does not understand what he must do, but then he realizes that "fix" can also mean fix in place, in which case he has no problem. This insight, despite Barth's modest disclaimer that he has little philosophical knowledge, sounds very much like one of Wittgenstein's primary contributions to philosophy: his theory that philosophical problems can be reduced to linguistic problems.

The next step in the replacement of everyday reality by a linguistic construct is to claim that a substantial part of human activity, much more than just human utterances, actually is linguistic. Near the end of *Giles Goat-Boy* Barth describes a committee that is trying to trace the history of "pass," "fail" and their derivatives, believing that "the history of certain such interpretations . . . could be said to figure the intellectual biography of studentom [mankind]" (p. 722). Here he claims that language has even more value for man, because it determines almost completely how people think and thereby determines to a large degree how they live. This theory naturally would appeal to a literary man, because it leads to the theory that reality is particularly amenable not only to language but also to media that rely on language, most notably, literature. After that one can easily say that language and literature *are* reality, and Barth has often but hesitantly made that assertion.

Although he became interested in metamorphosis not in the field and at the microscope studying butterflies, as did Nabokov, but probably in the classics library at Johns Hopkins reading mythology, Barth, too, is fascinated by this topic. This interest manifests itself mainly in his characterization. In "Menelaiad" Proteus himself appears, and two characters like him are in Barth's last two novels. Burlingame in *The Sot-Weed Factor,* through disguises, continually changes his appearance. Bray in *Giles Goat-Boy* at first poses as a Grand Tutor and near the end of the novel he ascends, metamorphosing as he does (p. 751). Polyeidus in "Bellerophoniad" and the gods in both that work and "Perseid" metamorphose. These Protean characters cast doubt on the concept of identity, another basic premise of realism.

The fictional world that Barth creates continually moves for another reason. He tries to show that people should be concerned with process, not with product. He makes this point in *Floating Opera* by means of the image of the showboat and its excellent construction. In contrast, Todd feels ashamed about the uncompleted boats he has tried to build, and he despairs about being able to finish his Inquiry. But he is wrong; construction in itself has value, more value than a finished product. The purpose in life, Barth suggests, is to make things well. The obscure ending of George's quest demonstrates the same point; he derives meaning merely by going on a quest, so he need not finish it. The main kind of process in Barth's work is artistic. Because of their meandering plots and talkative narrators his books seem to be open-ended, almost as if they were being created right before the reader.

Rather than developing some of the other positive themes that interest Borges and Nabokov, Barth expends an inordinate amount of energy on the theme of opposites. In fact, primarily by using this theme he at first examines the validity of realism and later moves beyond it to the Literature of Exhaustion. He works almost obsessively with this theme in *The Sot-Weed Factor* but uses it considerably less in his next three books, in which, oddly, his chosen mode better suits this theme. It took him a bit longer to learn how to apply his new techniques to this theme, so he handled it in the mode of the Literature of Exhaustion only after he had learned to handle other matters in this way. For these reasons the theme of opposites has a central position in these four books, and by tracing it through them one can see his development and, along the way, watch a typical movement toward the Literature of Exhaustion. In this case, ontogeny really does recapitulate phylogeny: Barth's development recapitulates the development of the Literature of Exhausion.

The importance of this theme lies in the fact that opposites are a category of thought, one of man's most common ways of organizing ideas and therefore one of the most important constituents of this world. Like space and time, realists use them to constitute their ideas of the world, so anti-realists must discredit them. At first Barth chose as a primary target the belief that things exist in simple pairs of opposites. His solution to the problem of opposites later became one of his most important positive themes.

In its simplest aspect the theme of opposites occurs in the characterization in *The Sot-Weed Factor*. The twinship of Eben and Anna permits a display of Barth's erudition in a chapter on the role and meaning of twins, and it also determines a good deal of their personalities. They are opposites by virtue of their difference in sex, yet their twinship suggests that they are also in some ways a unit. Their yearning for union resembles the androgynes' yearning in Aristophanes' myth in *The Symposium*, but it leads to incestuous desires, which occasionally become almost conscious. The union they seek they once had in "the dark identity that twins share in the womb" (p. 518). Anna's ring visually represents this union. Starting at one point and following the lettering around its circle, one reads, "a," "n," "n," "e," "b," which shows the entertwining of their names. Eben's flight from the incestuous implications of his desire to unite with Anna drives forward the plot early in the book. and their drifting back together drives the plot later.

Their twinship has a thematic dimension also, as its sexual meanings demonstrate. In an exaggerated form—partly because of the pervasive incest taboo—they demonstrate the desire of male and female to unite. This dimension should surprise no one, for "all men reverence the act of fornication as portraying the fruitful union of opposites" (p. 523). On the same page Barth refers to the connection of twins with coitus, which makes their representation of the union of male and female even more logical. This male and female theme takes many forms in *The Sot-Weed Factor*, most of them far less solemn and philosophical than this one that symbolizes the union of opposites. Many of these instances lack philosophical significance but have an almost Chaucerian gusto.

The twins represent other paired opposites besides male and female. According to Burlingame, they stand for the general principle of opposition. He claims that Eben and Anna are "the twin principles of male and female, mortal and divine, good and evil, light and darkness" (p. 521). These pairs are so basic and so nearly omnipresent that the world does indeed appear to be composed of opposites. Burlingame uses opposition as a category of thought, one that the bulk of the action in *The Sot-Weed Factor* validates. Many of the situations and the themes developed in this novel depend on pairs of opposites: America-Europe, innocence-experience, oppressed-oppressor, virginity-sexuality, and on and on. The pair of opposites that over-arches most of the others is, to state it in an extreme form, civilization and savagery. Part of a chapter title states this pair and asks a question vital to this novel: "Does essential savagery lurk beneath the skin of civilization, or does essential civilization lurk beneath the skin of savagery?" (p. 638).

If to a large extent paired opposites comprise the world, a person who wishes to function efficiently in it must learn to deal with them. At times Eben copes so badly with this problem that he cannot function at all. Like Jake Horner of *End of the Road*, he suffers from cosmopsis: being so baffled by the world that he cannot act, or sometimes even move. A vivid example of this malady appears in the scene at the bookseller's. Wanting to buy a notebook, he learns that four variables enter into the choice—thickness, presence or absence of lines, type of binding and size—and each variable has two opposite possibilities. The bookseller enumerates the possible combinations of these variables, which overwhelms Eben, who cannot choose between two opposites, much less among so many. Eben flees, physically to America and morally and psychologically to innocence, sexual and otherwise, because he cannot deal with opposites. In flight he at least achieves motion and escapes the immobility that afflicted him early in the book.

Burlingame deals much better than Eben with the problem of opposites, because he embraces both terms of any pair of opposites that he encounters. As to the characters and plot of the novel, he loves both Anna and Eben. "Embrace" is the appropriate word, because he does not love them Platonically; late in the book he admits to a physical desire for both twins. As to themes, he loves their twinship. His attitude toward them shows more than a liking for two people; it also reveals his philosophical orientation. He accurately describes himself as "Suitor of Totality, Embracer of Contradictories, Husband to all Creation, the Cosmic Lover" (p. 526). He can cope much better with the world than Eben can for he acts freely and accomplishes most of his goals, including the discovery of his ancestor's journal, through trickery and quick-wittedness. At the novel's end, however, he fades away into Indian territory, supposedly an unsuccessful man escaping as completely as possible from the world that he could not handle as well as he thought he could.

The norms of *The Sot-Weed Factor*, not the characters' beliefs, are vital. The final fate of Eben and Burlingame implies that according to Barth neither has the correct position on the question of opposites. Barth reveals his own position by the way he develops his themes, and he provides plenty of evidence because nearly all these themes can be paired into opposites. A reader can profitably begin by looking at a very basic theme, the male-female opposition. Eben believes, and appears to be correct, that avoiding sex will allow him to escape the flux of the world and its confusing opposites. But sex, by uniting opposites, will provide a victory over them, too. If both a method and its opposite work, the problem must be wrongly formulated. It is not clear whether Barth set out to show that opposites do not organize the world or whether he discovered it in the development of his themes, but this does not matter.

To sum up, Barth organizes this novel on the principle of opposition, then denies the validity of this principle. In so doing he accomplishes more than self-contradiction or what the scientists call negative proof, for, after all, something remains. The remnant can be called by the term he applies to *Roderick Random*, "adventurousness," or, better, it can be called *The Sot-Weed Factor*. In other words, he has difficulty with the problem of opposites, which implies that the realists who depend on this category of thought will inevitably have difficulty also and that realism is on the wrong track. But the very process of becoming balked leads toward the Literature of Exhaustion, for it turns out that he has written a book about the impossibility of writing a book on this basic principle of realism. Soon he was to discover that he could write a book about the impossibility of writing a book of any kind, at least an original book.

In *Giles Goat-Boy* he neither throws up his hands before the problem of opposites nor tries to solve it by uniting the pairs. Rather, he tries to transcend the pairs. George's assignments all require him to deal successfully with a pair of opposites, and the possible results of his handling of the assignments form the basic pair of the book, failure and passage. George, after passing through two earlier stages in his attitude toward this topic, the first like Eben's and the second like Burlingame's, finally decides to transcend opposites. Barth demonstrates that in this book he begins to master this problem, because, despite the importance of opposites to the conception of this novel, they do not appear nearly as frequently in its texture as they do in *The Sot-Weed Factor*. However, Barth advocates a less than satisfactory solution in *Giles Goat-Boy*, because it is philosophical. Not till *Lost in the Funhouse* does he solve the problem by aesthetic means, thereby getting himself in such a position that he need not deal with it anymore.

A reader can see the progress that George makes with this problem by comparing his three sets of answers to the computer's questions. Each time he has to answer these four questions: are you male or female? have you completed your assignment in no time? are you the Giles? and do you want to pass? During his first attempt he believes that absolutes and opposites exist, so he answers "yes" to each question (p. 561ff). At this point he asks himself, "what had my day's work proved, if not the necessity of clear distinction.

. . . To distinguish Tick from Tock, East Campus from West, Grand Tutor from goat, appearance from reality" (p. 535). Later he decides that absolutes do not exist and that therefore opposites are false, so he answers all the questions with "no" (p. 695ff). He gives the wrong answers both times, so he has to descend a third time into the belly of the computer and answer again.

This third and final set of answers agrees with the norms of the novel. This time George neither affirms nor denies the existence of absolutes and opposites, but rather asserts that "absolute" and "opposite" are false categories or, to use the Logical Positivists' term, he claims that he has been asked pseudo-questions. To put it another way, a more basic question underlies all four questions: "are x and y distinct and opposite?" George's successive answers to the four questions are equivalent to these answers to the basic question: "yes," "no," "your terms are nonsense." For him, "same" and "different," "true" and "false" and the terms that apply to questions in general, rather than to particular questions, the terms that people need in order to think, cannot be distinguished. In short, here Barth uses a philosophical involution—an examination of the basic, general conceptions of this discipline—that closely resembles the literary ones that the Literature of Exhaustion uses. All this lies behind George's answer of "yes" and "no" to each question.

Robert Scholes writes about Barth's final position on the matter of opposites in *Giles Goat-Boy*: "creation involves the kind of necessary and fruitful conflict symbolized by Yang and Yin and manifested in the sexual embrace" (p. 154). Thus, something that looks like a pair of opposites is really a combination of interdependent elements, the members of which are paradoxically both opposite and not opposite. This interpretation holds true even for the basic pair; as Scholes writes, "passage and failure are distinct but interdependent" (p. 167). George and Anastasia visually represent this idea by their position in the tapelift, which George describes: "knees to chin and arsy-turvy—like two shoes in a box, or that East-Campus sign of which her navel had reminded me" (p. 729). The East-

Campus sign represents Yang and Yin. In the two pages that follow this description George and Anastasia engage sexually in a "fruitful union of opposites" and George finds the Answer.

George's Answer and the answers he finally gives to the computer comprise the final step of a learning process that he undergoes as he tries to do his seven assignments. These assignments, too, force decisions about pairs of opposites, so they prepare him for his final insight. Most of the seven involve (a) an assignment, (b) a discipline, (c) an upholder of the false viewpoint about the assignment, (d) an answer and (e) a duality. These assignments are, One: (a) fix the clock in no time, (b) science, (c) Eierkopf, (d) it is fixed (accurate, fixed in position) and (e) tick and tock. Two: (a) end the boundary dispute, (b) politics, (c) Rexford, (d) it is an artificial dispute, and (e) East and West. Three: (a) overcome your infirmity, (b) philosophy, (c) Sear, (d) know yourself, (e) Grand Tutor and goat. Four: (a) see through your ladyship, (b) psychology, (c) Mrs. Sear, (d) "know" her, in the biblical sense of the word, (e) male and female. Five: (a) re-place the Founder's Scroll, (b) religion, (c) Virginia Hector, (d) it is *sui generis* and therefore needs its own place, (e) not a duality but a multiplicity (all possible literary categories). Because more than two categories relate to assignment five, the dualities start to break down by that time. Both assignments six and seven lack answers and dualities. Six: (a) pass the finals, (b) myth, (c) Bray. Seven: (a) present your i.d. card, (b) myth again, (c) Reginald Hector.

These assignments thus progress from duality to a transcendence of duality. Appropriately, there are concurrent progressions from rational categories to myth and from answers to a rising above answers. Like the three sets of answers that George gives to the computer, these progressions show that opposites are false categories. As he did in *The Sot-Weed Factor*, Barth tears down his premise—in this case, that absolutes and opposites exist—after he finishes with it. In *Giles Goat-Boy*, he ends up with more than a book, for he also arrives at an answer to the question of opposites, even though it is a philosophical answer.

In *Lost in the Funhouse* he takes the next and final step toward his solution of the problem of opposites, an artistic solution. In this book he eventually denies this theme in the only completely valid way that a writer can deny a theme, by declining to write about it. However, he begins in his book where he left off in *Giles Goat-Boy*. He returns to the problem of opposites in "Night-Sea Journey," a story published in 1966, the same year as *Giles Goat-Boy*. The tasks of the hero in the mythic plane (or plane of phylogeny) of this story are *"consummation, transfiguration, union of contraries, transcension of categories"* (p. 10). On another plane, ontogeny, opposites unite as they do in the earlier books, sexually, for on this plane the narrator is a sperm. On the plane of cosmogeny, which again equals literature, the goal is to pass beyond realism and its dependence on opposites. Barth does this by writing this book.

Barth's breakthrough comes in "Petition," which first appeared in *Lost in the Funhouse*, two years later than "Night-Sea Journey." Here he again uses twins to develop the theme of opposites, but he intensifies the problem by making the twins Siamese. The solution that worked in *Giles Goat-Boy* appears in a reference to the real Siamese twins Chang and Eng, the "veritable Heavenly Twins, sons of the mystical East, whose religions and philosophies . . . have ever minimized distinctions, denying even the difference between Sameness and Difference" (p. 57). The real transcendence, however, comes later when Barth forms another of his characteristic triangles by adding a lady acrobat, Thalia. He underscores the importance of this triangle by making it visual; the three characters form geometric designs as part of their carnival act. The role in mythology of Thalia represents the solution to the problem of opposites; she is the muse of comic and pastoral literature. Pastoral literature plays no part in this story, though it did in the capsule history of literature in *Giles Goat-Boy*. Her identification with comedy, however, does matter, because this identification means that a writer by controlling his tone and also the rest of his techniques can master the problem of opposites, or any other problem.

This happens in "Petition," for Barth there turns a potentially sad story—sad either because of the narrator's personal plight or because of his failure to deal successfully with opposites—into comedy. The addition of Thalia and what she represents thus acts like an exorcism for Barth, and he seems thereby finally to have mastered the problem of opposites. That is, one who has carefully followed Barth's handling of this theme through three books can see that Barth has shown the impossibility of writing literature based on opposites in a peculiar but logical way, by finally not writing that kind of literature. He does not use this theme at all in *Chimera*. This method comes after an early obsession with opposites and a later demonstration that realism cannot work with opposites. Barth thus arrives at the Literature of Exhaustion's position in regard to this theme also.

Childhood is a much less complicated and less persistent theme in his work than is opposition. After studying this theme in Nabokov's work, one can see Barth's development of it more clearly, since the two use the theme in almost identical ways. Like *Ada*, *The Sot-Weed-Factor* describes childhood as a paradise of incest. Burlingame draws this analogy with paradise for Eben, whose initial innocence and later experience resemble Adam's. Eben's father plays the wrathful God who expels the sinner from the garden. Richard Noland's interpretation of this subject in *The Sot-Weed Factor* also casts light on *Ada*: "The pure being that Ebenezer seeks, that state above death and time with which he concludes his hymn to innocence, may well be the paradaisal and timeless world of his and Anna's childhood" (p. 255). Barth makes childhood more conventional and less prominent in his next two books. In *Giles Goat-Boy* it is pastoral and Edenic but subsidiary to the allegory developed from George's early years. Ambrose's childhood typifies the hero's in *Bildungsromanen*.

In his works Barth usually treats positively the theme of sex. Like Nabokov, he considers it not an immersion in the real world but an escape from it. As he does with many of his themes, he develops this one in a logical progression from book to book. In *The Sot-Weed Factor* he presents a wide variety of sex; in fact, Burlingame alone has an almost pansexuality. Noland believes that Eben's lack of identity causes part of his sexual innocence (p. 251). Joseph more convincingly considers the cause and effect relation to be more complicated: "Eben's single-minded devotion to Joan Toast is now a cause, now an effect of his search for selfhood" (p. 28). In any case, Barth connects sex with identity in this novel, using it as a realistic novelist, interested in identity, would use it. In *Giles Goat-Boy*, however, he refers less frequently to sex in order to make a realistic point, or any point at all. Late in the novel it symbolizes the union of opposites, but earlier he merely describes it with great vigor. Scholes forcefully characterizes the effect of this treatment: "Barth's *Revised New Syllabus* comically but seriously reinstates the goatish side of man. George is . . . a saviour who will restore sexuality to an honored place in human existence" (p. 147). In *Lost in the Funhouse* he establishes the main function of sex in the first story, "Night-Sea Journey," in which it is a microcosm. He urges it to argue that the realists mistakenly conceive of the world, because they do not suspect the existence of the kind of order that a microcosm represents.

Barth shares with Borges and Nabokov the technique of developing these themes with characteristic, recurring imagery. He rarely uses Borges's favorite image, the labyrinth. It does appear in "Lost in the Funhouse" when he mentions the funhouse's labyrinthine corridors (p. 92). That structure, by the end of the story, symbolizes literature. "Labyrinthine" seems like an appropriate adjective for the intricate structures Barth creates for the reader, who often gropes along trying to follow them. In one of these labyrinthine corridors lies the skeleton of a man who had told himself stories while wandering in the funhouse, and whose stories had been recorded by an eavesdropper. This involution, turning back to describe the production of literature, is aptly represented by the image of the labyrinth, the correct path of which also doubles back on itself.

Like Borges and Nabokov, Barth describes many mirrors, even in his first novel, *The Floating Opera*. Todd sees his first sexual experience in the most prominent mirror in that book. Glimpsing the sex act in this way makes it appear comic to him. In other words, this mirror, like realistic literature, fairly accurately represents man, particularly his follies, to himself. By the time he wrote *Giles Goat-Boy* Barth had abandoned realism, and with it the conception he had of mirrors in *Floating Opera*. His symbol for realistic analysis becomes the lens and its variants like the scope and fluoroscope. Scholes explains in detail these images. In *Giles Goat-Boy* the character most out of touch with the real world, mainly because he accepts its reality, is Eierkopf, who also admits that mirrors and scopes are his favorite things (p. 379). Some of the other characters realize that mirrors usually distort like those in funhouses, in other words, that reality differs from its appearance. Max Spielman, one of the sages in the book, knows this all along, and Peter Greene realizes it after his failure to recognize it causes him a great deal of anguish. In Barth's next book the funhouse mirrors dominate and the funhouse itself becomes both the major image and the symbol of literature. Thus one sees from still another angle Barth's progressive disenchantment with realism and his progressive movement toward a classic variety of the Literature of Exhaustion.

This same growing disenchantment influences Barth's characterization. Aside from his self-consciousness as a narrator, Todd Andrews is realistic, as are the other characters in *Floating Opera*. In *End of the Road* the characters begin to lose some of their aura of reality as Barth manipulates them to make intellectual points, as the authors of anatomies manipulate their characters. Throughout his four most recent books Barth uses the same techniques that Borges and Nabokov use to attack the belief that fictional characters should be realistic, and thereby to attack obliquely the notion that actual people have real, consistent identities.

For example, to mount this attack he portrays characters as readers or writers, thereby gently pointing out their fictive nature and their inclusion in the illusory world of the novel. He unmistakably does not imitate actual people. Usually he inserts these points into the plot without jarring the reader. For instance, the list of the books that Eben Cooke likes and his poems that are scattered throughout the text seem to be perfectly natural details. A little more surprising, because it runs counter to the reader's knowledge of history, Barth presents John Smith's diary along with the implication that Smith should be known by what he has allegedly written, not by what historians tell us about him. In *Lost in the Funhouse* Barth cares much less about preserving verisimilitude and about making this point obliquely. Instead he jolts the reader with swift transitions between the real and fictive worlds. An example can be drawn from "Menelaiad":

" ' " ' " 'The death-horse dunged the town with Greeks; Menelaus ground his teeth, drew sword, changed point of view . . .' (p. 154)

Barth is even more fond than Borges and Nabokov of tricking his characters out in disguises. Burlingame continually disguises himself, and Barth sometimes does not explain these disguises until later in the novel, so that a reader always wonders whether a character is who he claims to be or just another avatar of Burlingame. Bray in *Giles Goat-Boy* also has mastered the art of disguise, but Barth always makes it clear whether or not Bray is in disguise. At one point George takes his cue from Bray and wears a mask that makes him look like Bray. Proteus in "Menelaiad" is the main user of disguises in *Lost in the Funhouse* and the mythological analogue of Burlingame and Bray. In "The Literature of Exhaustion" Barth casts light on the meaning of Proteus, and of the theme of disguise in general, by relating these matters to the tradition in which he is writing: "Homer's story in Book IV of the *Odyssey*, of Menelaus on the beach at Pharos, tackling Proteus, appeals profoundly to Borges: Proteus is he who 'exhausts the guises of reality' while Menelaus—who, one recalls, disguised his own identity in order to ambush him—holds fast" (p. 34).

Barth also creates doubles, another typical strategy of the Literature of Exhaustion. One would expect the first and third Burlingame to be doubles, and the first one's diary confirms that they are because it reveals that the later one has, in exaggerated form, the earlier one's problems with sex and with his identity. More surprising is the relation between John Smith and Eben, which even the usually unperceptive Eben recognizes: "once Ebenezer had wrested the *Secret Historie* from his memory he could not but marvel at the parallel between John Smith's experience and their own" (p. 559). These two pairs of characters fall short of being conventional doubles because of their close resemblance. One must go to *Giles Goat-Boy* to find pairs who fit more closely the strict meaning of doubles, and in that book they abound: George and Bray, two claimants to Grand Tutorhood; Eierkopf, nearly all mind, and his companion Croaker, nearly all body; Rexford, the accommodating, evasive liberal, and Stoker, the power-mad authoritarian. Barth uses this theme for two purposes. The creation of doubles implies that identity is a false category: if two people are alike, or in a simplified double relationship, neither has a unique, well defined identity of his own. A realist would counter by saying that even membership in a double confers identity, but Barth refutes this claim by dissolving, late in *Giles Goat-Boy*, the double relations in that book. Rexford becomes less manipulative and more coercive, like Stoker; Eierkopf in the clock tower turns brutish like Croaker; and Bray and George first reverse appearances by putting on masks in the other's likeness and then drift out of the book without making it clear which one, if either, is the Grand Tutor.

Barth also makes it obvious that his characters are fictive. He makes most of them flat and stereotyped, especially those from minorities, like Indians, Blacks and Jews. Scholes puts it another way by saying that in *Giles Goat-Boy* the "characters are closer to pre-novelistic kinds of characterization than to the deep individuality of the realists" (p. 160). Occasionally Barth has a character announce his fictiveness so that a reader cannot miss it. George says, "a fact, . . . even an autobiographical fact, was not something I perceived and acknowledged, but a detail of the general Conceit, to be accepted or rejected" (p. 117). At least once, in *The Sot-Weed Factor*, a character also draws the appropriate conclusion for the reader, the one that all of these techniques of characterization support. Burlingame claims, " 'all assertions of *thee* and *me*, e'en to oneself, are acts of faith, impossible to verify' " (p. 143).

Barth's plots attack the notions of causality and time, rather than depending on them, as the realists' plots do. He links the actions together in haphazard fashion, and characters meet usually not because their destinies bring them together but because of coincidence. The plots also lack internal consistency. In *The Sot-Weed Factor* he is especially oblivious to consistency; some of its characters even die and then reappear later. The enormous complexity of Barth's plots makes it nearly impossible for anyone to understand them, even if he could depend on traditional organizing devices like the conception of cause and effect. In his interview in *Wisconsin Studies* Barth mentions that one of his major goals in writing *The Sot-Weed Factor* "was to see if [he] couldn't make up a plot that was fancier than *Tom Jones*" (p. 7). If there were some scale by which to measure plot complexity it very likely would turn out that his plot is indeed fancier than Fielding's.

Little has been written about Barth's style, less than his artistry merits. Most critics who have discussed *The Sot-Weed Factor* have pointed out its obvious imitation of eighteenth century style but have not probed too deeply into the meaning of this tour de force. His style in that book, being anachronistic, calls attention to itself and therefore announces the artifice of literature. Two stylistic analyses, however, provide some help. Robert Scholes, near the beginning of his chapter on *Giles Goat-Boy*, looks at Barth's style, and, though he moves a bit too quickly to analysis of theme, he does provide some insights about the style of this book. Perhaps the best clue to Barth's style appears in Richard Schickel's article on *The Floating Opera*; he says that Barth writes in "a wayward, quirky, but highly charged style in which the conversational varies with the formal, the flowery with the direct, the vulgar with the sensitive."[11]

This mixture of stylistic opposites rings a bell, since the theme of opposites dominates Barth's works. The most interesting feature of Barth's style, then, is that it reinforces a major theme. A reader can most easily see how he does this, and note other important aspects of his style, by carefully analyzing representative passages from his work. The openings of books, because writers usually meticulously fashion them, make good subjects. One must remember that Barth continually changes his style to suit his purpose; for example, the occasionally legalistic prose of *The Floating Opera* fits Todd Andrews. Thus, analysis will often reveal only how his style works at a particular point. After setting aside the introductory matter of *Giles Goat-Boy*, the first paragraph of the First Reel becomes a logical choice for analysis:

> George is my name; my deeds have been heard of in Tower Hall, and my childhood has been chronicled in the *Journal of Experimental Psychology*. I am he that was called in those days Billy Bocksfuss—cruel misnomer. For had I indeed a cloven foot I'd not now hobble upon a stick or need ride pick-a-back to class in humid weather. Aye, it was just for want of a proper hoof that in my fourteenth year I was the kicked instead of the kicker; that I lay crippled in the reeking peat and saw my first love tupped by a brute Angora. Mercy on that buck who butted me from one world to another; whose fell horns turned my sweetheart's fancy, drove me from the pasture, and set me gimping down the road I travel yet. This bare brow, shame of my kidship, he crowned with the shame of men: I bade farewell to my hornless goathood and struck out, a hornèd human student, for Commencement Gate. (p. 41)

Barth's use here of the smallest unit of style, sound, calls attention to itself, as in the jawbreaking combination of hard consonants in "crippled on the reeking peat." Natural in poetry, alliteration often distracts in prose, so it, too, calls attention to itself. He uses it a few times in the paragraph, twice in the last sentence: "bare brow" and "hornèd human." Also, his alliteration lends a sense of energy to his prose by intensifying some of the accents and breaking up the smooth flow. He rarely uses other poetic devices; he writes not poetic prose but unusual prose.

At the level of words his creation of opposites begins to become more apparent. Until one recognizes the relation of his stylistic opposites to his development of the theme of opposites, he seems to be working at cross purposes. Besides the strange apparatus that opens *Giles Goat-Boy*, a few expressions in this paragraph are peculiar enough to bother a reader. Barth has cleverly placed one, "Tower Hall," at the beginning and another, "Commencement Gate," at the very end. He gives no explanation of these terms and the strange story of the part-human goat that makes up the subject matter of the paragraph certainly is not reassuringly familiar. At the same time—literally at the same time as the first instance of peculiarity, since it, too, appears in the first sentence—he creates an air of verisimilitude, the opposite effect. He alludes to the *Journal of Experimental Psychology*, the apparent authenticity and scientific respectability of which encourage the reader to believe the story that will follow. If a journal like that reported it, it surely must be true. Barth's ploy resembles Swift's elaborate creation of an air of authenticity in the opening of *Gulliver's Travels*, which also has many unfamiliar and exotic expressions.

The levels of diction in this paragraph also exhibit a pair of opposites. It has an archaic flavor, created in part by "aye" and "bade." More striking, he uses the archaic "for want of a proper hoof." This phrase sounds like eighteenth century prose, as if Barth has a few stylistic tricks left over from *The Sot-Weed Factor*. He produces a similar effect with two fancy words: "chronicled" where "discussed" or even "told" would do, and "misnomer." At the other extreme he uses two strikingly blunt words: the vividly effective slang "gimping" and "tupped." The effectiveness of the latter term is typical of Barth; he has perhaps the world's largest collection of synonyms for that term and always chooses the one that best fits his context and texture.

The aforementioned energy contributes one member of still another pair of opposites. Besides the alliteration, one of his less important methods of achieving this effect, he uses devices that bring him dangerously close to over-writing. For instance, he converts verbs into other parts of speech in order to make the passage seem full of action. "Kicked," "kicker," and "crippled" accomplish

this. Frequent over-statement raises the energy level of the prose
in a different way. Within a few lines appear "reeking peat," "but-
ted me from one world to another" and "shame of my kidship."
But he also shows a good deal of restraint. One of the strongest
temptations to the flowery writer is to overuse adjectives, but Barth
uses a fairly low percentage of them and for the most part avoids
distractingly colorful ones. In fact, the percentage of the parts of
speech in this paragraph must be close to typical.

The most common figures of speech—symbols, metaphors, and
similes, for instance—rarely appear in this passage. Very many of
them added to the exotic things described here in a straightforward
manner would stretch too far a reader's suspension of disbelief, or
his power of comprehension. In other words, it would be overwhelming to invent a metaphor to describe the "hornèd human student."
Unlike the mundane scarcity of figures of speech, his allusions are
plentiful. One source is moderately surprising, the other somewhat
startling. The first allusion, the German "Bocksfuss," does not quite
mean the cloven foot that Barth implies but rather ram's foot. In
any case, one would not expect to go to a German dictionary while
reading the first paragraph of this novel. Two phrases have even
more peculiar sources: "I am he that was called" and "crowned
with the shame of men." Their biblical ring, however, suits the book
that Barth has called a comic Old Testament.

Another set of opposites appears in the next largest unit of style,
phrases and sentences. He often clips the former, reducing them
to the absolute minimum number of words that will express the
requisite idea, like "I'd not now hobble." Its sound—the alliteration
and assonance—and the rhythm—the four hard accents followed
by one soft one—create a subtle melding of sound and sense. The
style produces a hobbling effect rather like Richard Wilbur's in
the opening of "Death of a Toad": "A frog with a hobbling hop."
Despite this attribute of Barth's phrases, his sentences are the
opposite of clipped. They average about twenty-eight words, quite
high for a passage describing action in a novel, and they gracefully
move. He even writes stately inverted sentences. In addition to

their length his sentences are intricately put together, often in a parallel fashion. Although this passage has only six sentences, it makes Barth, because of the variety of his sentence types, seem like a virtuoso writer at this level.

This passage from *Giles Goat-Boy*, though only one paragraph, demonstrates that Schickel's point about the opposites in the style of *The Floating Opera* holds true also for some of Barth's later work. One should not use Schickel's term "quirky" in a pejorative sense. Barth does have an unusual style, but the real issue is its effectiveness. It can serve best by reinforcing the effect created by the other elements of fiction in a given work. This Barth has managed, imposing his vision on his material so completely that he has produced a work whose elements all interact to create a unified effect.

One can double-check the hypothesis that Barth's style reinforces his theme and that it relates particularly to his handling of the theme of opposites by looking at another passage from a story in which Barth develops this theme differently. The best choice is "Petition," the story in which he symbolizes, by means of Thalia, a satisfactory way to handle opposites. Unlike many of the other works in *Lost in the Funhouse*, it does not have so many involuted devices that one finds the prose nearly impossible to analyze. The story takes the form of a letter written by an imaginary character, but this does not diminish its appropriateness as an object of stylistic analysis. Again, the beginning of the work provides the best sample, though the heading and very brief first paragraph of the letter are irrelevant here. This is the second paragraph:

> Though not myself a native of your kingdom, I am and have been most alive to its existence and concerns—unlike the average American, alas, to whose imagination the name of that ancient realm summons only white elephants and blue-eyed cats. I am aware, for example, that it was Queen Rambai's father's joke that he'd been inside the Statue of Liberty but never in the United States, having toured the Paris foundry while that symbol was a-casting; in like manner I may say that I have dwelt in a figurative Bangkok all my life. My brother,

with whose presumption and other faults I hope further to acquaint you in the course of this petition, has even claimed (in his cups) descent from the mad King Phaya Takh Sin, whose well-deserved assassination—like the surgical excision of a cataract, if I may be so bold—gave to a benighted land the luminous dynasty of Chakkri, whereof Your Majesty is the latest and brightest son. Here as elsewhere my brother lies or is mistaken: we are Occidental, for better or worse, and while our condition is freakish, our origin is almost certainly commonplace. Yet though my brother's claim is false and (should he press it upon you, as he might) in contemptible taste, it may serve the purpose of introducing to you his character, my wretched situation, and my petition to your magnanimity. (pp. 55–56)

The opposite qualities of style that Schickel finds in *Floating Opera* and that I find in the first paragraph of *Giles Goat-Boy* proper do not exist in this passage from "Petition." The style here does call attention to itself, as it did in the other passage, but by its tone, not by devices of sound that are more common in poetry. The sound obtrudes only in the repetition in "latest and brightest," an unstriking example. Rather, this passage's carefully embellished style and its highly civilized tone make it so clearly an artifice. This passage has a Nabokovian dandyism about it. In fact, this quality, in addition to its desperate yet genteel narrator and its building of a fairy kingdom, make it read like an excerpt from one of Nabokov's novels. This dandyism could be balanced by bluntness to form another style built on opposites—after all, this narrator has a tupping of his loved one by his Siamese twin to describe—but it is not.

This dandyism of style appears mainly in the diction: words like "alas," "contemptible," "magnanimity," and "mistaken," all of which could be omitted or replaced by less flowery words. Phrases like "if I may be so bold" and "in his cups" are similar. This fancy diction serves two functions. First, it heightens the comedy by contrasting the narrator's verbal skill with his inept handling of everything else. Nabokov does this also, for example in Humbert's "I have only words to play with." Second, it helps characterize the narrator. Because of his oppression he has developed a protective timidity, which appears in the bathos of "my brother lies or is mistaken." This passage contains many more adjectives than does the passage from *Giles Goat-Boy,* and the ones here are more imaginative. One brief section has two effective adjectives: "gave to a benighted land the luminous dynasty." No blunt words contrast with these fancy ones, and few verbals balance the important adjectives; the style here is contemplative, not active.

Unlike the other passage, this one contains similes and metaphors, including two very effective ones: the comparison of an assassination to a "surgical excision of a cataract" and of the conditions of the narrator's life to a "figurative Bangkok." Also unlike the other passage, this one has no apparent allusions. Yet his sensitive, articulate narrator should occasionally invent apt tropes. Again, regarding this aspect of style, Barth uses no pairs of opposites.

Besides the fancy phrases mentioned earlier, Barth uses some circumlocutions, like "I may say," "the course of," and "serve the purpose of." His sentences are also somewhat baroque. They average about forty-seven words, over half-again as long as the sentences in the other passage. The absence of action causes part, but far from all, of this increase in length. Like the other passage, this one has sentence variety and parallelism. The intricacy of the sentence construction has increased. For example, he puts together the third sentence in real virtuoso fashion, meandering, though with impeccable logic, from the narrator's brother to the King. The clipped, economical phrases that he used in this type of sentence in the other passage rarely occur this time, so once again his style here produces a unified effect.

Both the attention-getting quality of Barth's style and its efficient reinforcement of the other elements of his fiction typify the Literature of Exhaustion. The former quality helps create the artifice of this kind of literature. The latter quality makes a work more unified and self-enclosed, cut off definitely from the real world rather than being a model of it. And of course Barth shares these qualities with Borges and Nabokov.

Barth also combats the realists on the battleground of point-of-view. Rejecting more sophisticated ways to divide this element of fiction into categories, he uses the common one of first-person and third-person and shows that this can be a false distinction. By doing this he proves that point of view is much more complex than most realists suspect. His most subtle proof of this complexity appears in "Echo." Gerhard Joseph has explained it in an intricate discussion that requires extensive quotation:

> "Echo" . . . accomplishes the complete amalgamation of the first-and third-person point of view. Narcissus seems to be the speaker, telling his familiar tale in the third person to Tiresias as an antidote to self-love: "One does well," the story opens, "to speak in the third person, the seer advises, in the manner of Theban Tiresias. A cure for self-absorption is saturation: telling the story over as though it were another's until like a much repeated word it loses sense." As Narcissus explores this perspective, lapsing at one point into the first person within the first person, we are led to suspect that the speaker may be either Tiresias or Echo, in which case the identity of the interlocutor is just as doubtful. While the narrative line is relatively clear because of the myth's familiarity, it becomes impossible to distinguish teller from listener and, ultimately, narrative from narrator. (p. 42)

The reader has even more difficulty making distinctions about this story than Joseph claims, for Narcissus is not the only one who "sees the nymph [Echo] efface herself until she becomes no more than her voice" (p. 98). The reader sees the same thing. In this effacement Barth presents his ultimate quibble with conventional ideas about point of view. He no longer denies only the distinction between first and third persons; he denies the distinction between point of view as a whole and character. He also suggests that everything else in a story can become subservient to a narrative voice. He makes the same suggestion in "Menelaiad": "this isn't the voice of Menelaus; this voice *is* Menelaus" (p. 127). Then he builds so many Chinese boxes in this story that the reader begins to believe this statement by and about the narrative voice.

To pare away the elements of fiction an author can next eliminate the narrative voice, by having the story tell itself. This supposedly happens in "Autobiography." Despite the interest, perhaps even the originality of this strategy, executing it does not take much skill, certainly much less than the skill with which Barth handles the point of view in "Echo." This idea as it appears in "Autobiography" can be visualized as a series of Chinese boxes. The outermost ones are again the author and the work. Then comes the narrative voice, according to Barth the ground of any story, and then the actual content of the story. Lately he has been trying to work outward from this last box, destroying each box as he goes until he leaves only the work and himself. That is, he would like to create a story called "Autobiography" that has no content and that would be like a Platonic form of a story. He creates a finite system of boxes in this story, since no other boxes can be built that will encompass the last one. This project sounds like some of Beckett's attempts to make do without various elements of fiction. More generally, to use this strategy a writer of the Literature of Exhaustion must first admit that literature is dead. Then he tries to prove this charge by destroying literature's constituents—while writing stories.

Like Borges and Nabokov, Barth adds a big dose of the leaven of comedy to make his heavy ingredients lighter and more airy. Not by accident, these three writers have in common both a particular kind of literature and great wit. The very nature of their mode requires and encourages a light comic touch. Scholes's term for the writers he analyzes, fabulators, means almost the same thing as the term I am using for these three writers. His statement about his writers holds also for Borges, Barth and Nabokov (and of course he includes Barth in his group, too): "fabulation . . . seems to partake of the comic" (p. 171). Again at the risk of choosing one that is not funny, a critic can give a sense of an author's comedy only by providing an example. A brief passage in "Echo" has several witticisms, some quite subtle, and a neat linguistic mirror that reinforces the visual scene being described: "like the masturbatory adolescent, sooner or later [Narcissus] finds himself. He beholds and salutes his pretty alter ego in the pool; in the pool his ego, altered, prettily salutes: Behold! In vain he reaches to embrace his contrary image; he recognizes what Tiresias couldn't warn him of. Has knowing himself turned him into a pansy?" (p. 99). Barth's comedy does not always occur in such a series or in such subtlety, but it pervades his work.

In many ways, then, Barth is a classic writer of the Literature of Exhaustion, but a tendency in his work, his growing interest in the theme of love, has allowed him to keep in touch with realism. However, he frequently takes an ironic attitude toward this theme. His first two, realistic novels depend quite heavily on the love theme, *The Floating Opera* more heavily than it first appears. Todd contemplates suicide not because of his philosophical impasse or even his awareness of his body brought on by Jane Mack's unintentionally disturbing remark about his peculiar fingers. Rather, her remark and his resulting temporary impotence—a condition that has been periodically bothering him—in conjunction force him to set aside his mask of cynicism and realize that he loves her. Todd will not admit this feeling in his narration and probably does not admit it to the higher centers of his consciousness, but Barth makes it clear that only this motive will explain Todd's actions. Thus, this philosophical novel actually turns on the issue of love. The love theme in *End of the Road*, although more crucial, is also so straightforward that it need not be explained here. However, both Todd and Jake Horner love in strange, impersonal ways.

In *The Sot-Weed Factor* love plays an important part. Through most of this novel it is subordinate to other themes like innocence, timelessness and opposites. At the very end, however, it comes to the forefront and the novel ends with a dénouement like a Shakespearian comedy's in which everyone marries. In Barth's novel, however, another unraveling occurs when the matches begin to dissolve, which ironically undercuts this theme. The love theme in *Giles*

Goat-Boy is almost identical. Through most of this novel it conveys the ideas that Barth wants to examine. At the end, the relation between George and Anastasia becomes paramount, and the techniques of the Literature of Exhaustion give way to the conventional novelistic techniques that are usually used to develop love themes.

Lost in the Funhouse depends throughout on the love theme and does not subordinate it to other concerns. The cry of " 'love, love, love' " that ends the first story, "Night-Sea Journey," echoes throughout the book. Often the love is unrequited, as in "Petition," or vicarious, as in "Water-Message," but these varieties are no less real. This theme plays an even more important part in two other stories. In "Menelaiad" Menelaus learns that he must placate not Athena, the goddess of wisdom, but Aphrodite, the goddess of love. Moreover, after one unpeels all the layers of this story, the core, the love story of Menelaus and Helen, becomes visible. "Ambrose His Mark" ends with the main character admitting his attitude toward the experiences he has just had:

> He wishes he had never entered the funhouse. But he has. Then he wishes he were dead. But he's not. Therefore he will construct funhouses for others and be their secret operator—though he would rather be among the lovers for whom funhouses are designed. (p. 94)

This is the subterranean message of *Lost in the Funhouse*.

In *Chimera* Barth treats love ironically. He compares sex so often with narration that the former theme becomes less important in itself than as a metaphor for the latter theme. For example, he says of the genie and Scheherazade " 'this last comparison—a favorite of theirs—would lead them to a dozen others between narrative and sexual art' " (p. 24). Moreover, Barth's technical experiments so dominate this book that the love relations in it lose their credibility and immediacy. This irony prevails in spite of the autobiographical implications of this theme in *Chimera*. In sum, it looks as if Barth will not use the theme of love to lead him back toward realism, but will instead continue his interest in the aesthetic themes of the Literature of Exhaustion.

One can more easily evaluate his work than Borges's and Nabokov's because Barth's is less diverse and less abundant. His nonfiction is less important than his fiction. "Muse, Spare Me," the afterword to *Roderick Random* and his essay on the Eastern Shore of Maryland, although interesting, are not ambitious. "The Literature of Exhaustion," however, is clearly one of the most provocative recent essays on literature, codifying for the first time an important school of writing. On a smaller scale but like *Axel's Castle*, *The Romantic Image* and *American Renaissance*, it maps new territory. It would be a boon if he would write more works like this. He and some other contemporary writers famous mainly for their fiction —like Updike and Mailer—write excellent literary criticism, bringing to this field the knowledge of the insider and the freshness of the master prose stylist.

Since his seminal essay he has deepened his understanding of the Literature of Exhaustion. He has begun to allude specifically in his fiction to the basic premise of this kind of literature. Dunyazade complains to Shah Zaman that " 'you've had the whole literary tradition transmitted to you' " (p. 32). Thus, she faces the same predicament as do writers like Barth. Barth, in the guise of the genie in "Dunyazadiad" hopes to solve this problem, "to go beyond [his past works] toward a future they were not attuned to and, by some magic, at the same time go back to the original springs of narrative" (p. 10). He does this in *Chimera* by using myths to communicate the contemporary writer's plight. Specifically, he proposes cryptically that "the key to the treasure is the treasure," that one can write in the face of this condition by writing *about* this condition. He also writes about Scheherazade because she desperately fought against a diminution of narrative possibilities in order to save her own life. The anguish of the contemporary writer took for Barth the form of a writer's block, but he later realized that the same solution would work " 'as soon as I understood that my writer's block was a precise metaphor for the story I was trying to write, the problem solved itself, the story came out in a burst.' "[12] In short, he has publicly demonstrated more awareness than Borges or Nabokov that he belongs to the Literature of Exhaustion, though the lack of statements by the latter two does not mean that they do not know what they are doing.

Until he produces more nonfiction, though, his reputation will rest on his novels and short stories. This work has obvious merits, such as the skill with which he uses words. He also clearly deserves credit for his wit and for his experiments. His detractors usually make the same complaints: that he is dull and that he is bloodless, magisterially and endlessly ruminating on trivial issues and turning his back on the real problems of his era. One cannot argue about dullness, except to say that lack of understanding sometimes causes boredom. Critics also make the second charge against Borges and Nabokov. Defending Barth on these grounds is a bit easier, because of his first two novels. Their realism and the problems they deal with make them the kind of novel admired by detractors of Barth's four most recent works, and this puts those detractors in an awkward position.

The position of these detractors becomes even more awkward when they see the connection between his first two works and his others. He deals with a wide range of interrelated problems in *Floating Opera* and *End of the Road*, but, inevitably, finds the full panoply too complex to admit of any solutions. In his later works he assumes that the aesthetic problems that he considers relevant are paradigmatic of the other problems, and he tries to wage his battle on only one front, giving himself a better chance of success. Both his subsidiary theme of love and his many connections of aesthetic matters with other matters indicate that he has never forgotten the problems that he has temporarily placed in abeyance. He worries about more than aesthetic ultimacy; he writes in "Title": "Everything's finished. Name eight. Story, novel, literature, art, humanism, humanity, the self itself" (p. 104). He also has faith that victory on one front will be decisive, for the next sentence is "Wait: the story's not finished" (p. 104). And it is not, and neither is Barth, and at least for a while neither is humanity.

In other words, Barth chooses reasonable grounds on which to withstand ultimacy. If one grants him his artistic goals and methods—either because of these arguments or because they should be granted to all writers—one can evaluate the products that he makes with them. *Floating Opera* is a first-rate novel, a remarkable work for a twenty-five year old writer. It has both obvious strengths—stylistic and thematic—and latent subtleties, some of which I have made manifest. *End of the Road* is notable mainly for the rapidity with which it followed its predecessor, for both were written during 1955. Otherwise it makes only a very slight advance in technique. It also has some flaws, mainly inconsistencies, like the characterization of Joe as both genius and dunce.

Next Barth switched to his later mode, though he did not completely abandon his earlier mode. *The Sot-Weed Factor*, probably the most enjoyable of his books, perhaps lacks the depth of others, and aside from its stylistic performance, it is not as innovative or technically interesting as some of his other books. *Giles Goat-Boy* brings to fruition the seeds sown in *The Sot-Weed Factor*. It has a certain woodenness but the other aspects of its technique include many genuinely new developments, and it has more philosophical depth than its predecessor. The first appearances of the stories in *Lost in the Funhouse* range over five years, falling both before and after *Giles Goat-Boy*. A few of them seem like five-finger exercises, trying out technical ideas on a small scale. Many of the stories, however, have merit, either technically, like "Menelaiad," or by conventional standards, like "Ambrose His Mark," or on both counts like "Lost in the Funhouse" and "Echo." Its unity adds strength to it and makes it a collection of carefully interrelated stories in the tradition of *Go Down, Moses* and *Winesburg, Ohio*, a tradition that unfortunately has not been kept up very well lately. In *Chimera* he further refines his techniques, but to do so he repeats aspects of his earlier works. The first two of the novellas deserve high marks, but "Bellerophoniad" sometimes drags.

In summary, Barth's fiction earns a high place. His work, especially *Floating Opera*, has found readers, though fewer than it should have. He has too few readers perhaps because he has too few critics: the longest analysis of his work aside from this one is Joseph's forty-page pamphlet, and the essays about him are mainly book reviews and therefore almost inevitably ephemeral. His work bears a great deal of careful explication and merits further attention.

Conclusion

In my brief evaluations of Borges, Nabokov, and Barth I have been concerned mainly with the intrinsic value of their works, with the quality of the individual works of literature that they have produced under the banner of the Literature of Exhaustion. Now that this literary movement has been somewhat clarified, however, it is appropriate to consider the value of the movement itself, to step back and view this literature from a broader perspective and to consider, in a more philosophical manner, the possible effect on literature, criticism, and culture of the basic principles and techniques of the Literature of Exhaustion. Taking such a broad view attributes a good deal of significance to this literature—broad perspectives do not suit minor writers—but Borges, Nabokov, and Barth merit this kind of treatment.

Other writers can best use the work of Borges, Nabokov, and Barth by learning from it that they can base literature on a conception of reality. Many writers of course have done this, but rarely with the rigor displayed by the Literature of Exhaustion. In other words, Borges, Nabokov, and Barth carefully derive their secondary themes and their techniques from their central metaphysical hypothesis. In his most recent work Barth has found interesting ways to communicate his basic ideas by means of his techniques, to make every element of his work "emblematic." While thus connecting form and content these three writers have invented new techniques and refined old ones, perhaps most notably by intricately developing the Chinese box technique. Because they concentrate a good deal of their energy on exploring literature's relation to everyday reality, they have cast some light on the nature of literature.

In other words, the probing of Borges, Nabokov, and Barth has located an escape from the dead end in which fiction finds itself. They can best proceed, however, by pulling back rather than pushing forward in the same direction. That is, producing more involuted literature may very well be redundant as far as the history of the genre goes, although interesting and significant individual works may result. It would be better to assimilate new techniques while at the same time keeping the best of the old-fashioned themes and techniques and refusing to renounce fiction's role of communicating a variety of significant ideas about human existence. To be specific, to some extent *Ada* and to a greater extent *Transparent Things* cover sufficiently well trodden ground. In contrast, *Pale Fire* and *Lolita* exhibit both interesting experiments and impressive insights into man, thus fulfilling the two goals that in "The Literature of Exhaustion" Barth proposes for contemporary literature. In short, fiction, whether it is dying or not, needs self-examination now, but not endless self-examination to the exclusion of other concerns. As Nabokov, and to a certain extent the other two, have shown, the Literature of Exhaustion has on occasion fulfilled both goals, an unusual achievement in contemporary literature.

Critics, too, can learn from the Literature of Exhaustion. The precision with which form fits content in this literature indicates how practical criticism can better follow this theoretical dictum. For example, a critic can trace the ways in which Borges's characterizations reinforce his opinions about identity and about common-sense notions of reality. Then such a critic will perhaps be more likely to relate character to the other elements of fiction. Even more significant, the Literature of Exhaustion indicates critical work that needs to be done. Our definitions lack the exactness needed to clarify completely this kind of literature. For instance, sophisticated critics have spent a good deal of energy refining our conception of point of view, but the stories in *Lost in the Funhouse* indicate that we need to go further. Moreover, we need to invent a term for the element of fiction to which the Chinese box technique belongs. The boxes are not a kind of structure because these writers do not sequentially describe the layers. "Levels of reality" fits reasonably well, but it is not a commonly accepted literary term.

The Literature of Exhaustion will not cure all cultural problems, since literature can offer solutions only to those problems that can be articulated in language. Calls for relevance in the restrictive, currently fashionable sense fall on particularly deaf ears when they are directed toward Borges, Nabokov, and Barth. However, because many disciplines, nonartistic as well as artistic, have entered a period of introspection, this type of literature may offer some clues about how these other disciplines can move forward more rapidly.

In summary, the Literature of Exhaustion is a fascinating and healthy development, particularly when a writer can use its innovations rather than be used by them. I have not come even close to saying the last word on these three writers or on others who can be considered with them. We need criticism of the Literature of Exhaustion that will have the erudition of Borges, the verbal facility of Nabokov, and the vigor of Barth.

Notes

Introduction

1. *Atlantic*, 220: 2 (August, 1967), 29–34. They have made a few references to each other. Barth on Nabokov: "John Barth: An Interview," *Wisconsin Studies in Contemporary Literature*, 6: 1 (Winter–Spring, 1965), 5; *TriQuarterly*, 17 (Winter 1970), 350. Nabokov on Borges: "Vladimir Nabokov: An Interview," *Paris Review*, 41 (Summer–Fall, 1967, 105; "An Interview with Vladimir Nabokov," *Nabokov: The Man and His Work* (Madison: University of Wisconsin Press, 1967), p. 34; "Prospero's Progress," *Time*, 93: 21 (May 23, 1969), 83; passing references to Borges as Osberg in *Ada*. Nabokov on Barth: "Inspiration," *Saturday Review*, 55: 47 (January, 1973), 32. A few critics have also grouped two or all three of them. On Borges and Nabokov: Patricia Merivale, "The Flaunting of Artifice in Vladimir Nabokov and Jorge Luis Borges," *Nabokov: The Man and His Work*, pp. 209–224; Alfred Appel, *Annotated Lolita* (New York: McGraw-Hill, 1970), passim; Ronald Christ, *The Narrow Act* (New York: New York University Press, 1969), passim; Gene Baliff, "Reading, Writing, and Reality," *Salmagundi*, 12 (Spring, 1970), 24–42. Nabokov and Barth: Julian Moynahan, *Vladimir Nabokov* (Minneapolis: University of Minnesota Press, 1970), pp. 31–32. All three: Gerhard Joseph, *John Barth* (Minneapolis: University of Minnesota Press, 1970), p. 30.

2. *Partisan Review*, 35: 1 (Winter, 1968), 13–27.

3. "The Aesthetics of Silence," *Styles of Radical Will* (New York: Dell Publishing Company, 1970), pp. 3–34.

4. New York: Atheneum, 1967.

5. New York: Alfred A. Knopf, 1967; New York: Oxford University Press, 1971.

6. Ihab Hassan, ed., *Liberations* (Middletown, Conn.: Wesleyan University Press, 1971), pp. 176–196.

7. *The Performing Self* (New York: Oxford University Press, 1971).

8. New York: Oxford University Press, 1967.

9. *The Field of Nonsense* (London: Chatto and Windus, 1952), p. 3.

10. "The American Novelist as Entropologist," *The London Magazine*, 10: 7 (October, 1970), 5–18. He develops this idea more fully in *City of Words*.

Jorge Luis Borges

1. New York: E. P. Dutton, 1972. Carter Wheelock describes the recent changes in Borges' work in "Borges' New Prose," *TriQuarterly*, 25 (Fall, 1972), 403–440.

2. "Profiles," 46: 31 (September 19, 1970), 40–99.

3. "An interview with Jorge Luis Borges," *Contemporary Literature*, 11: 3 (Summer, 1970), 323.

4. Afterword of *Dr. Brodie's Report*, p. 123.

5. "The Author as Librarian," *New Yorker*, 41: 37 (October 30, 1965), 223.

6. *Borges: The Labyrinth Maker* (New York: New York University Press, 1965), p. 38.

7. *The Narrow Act* (New York: New York University Press, 1969), p. 35.

8. *Jorge Luis Borges* (New York: Twayne, 1970), p. 59.

9. "Jorge Luis Borges: An Interview," *Paris Review*, 40 (Winter–Spring, 1967), 145.

10. In *Nabokov: The Man and His Work*, ed. L. S. Dembo (Madison: University of Wisconsin Press, 1967), pp. 209–224.

11. "Up From Ultraism," *New York Review of Books*, 15: 3 (August 13, 1970), 4.

12. Austin: University of Texas Press, 1969.

13. *Conversations With Jorge Luis Borges* (New York: Holt, Rinehart and Winston, 1969), p. 129.

14. "A Modern Master," *New York Review of Books*, 3: 7 (November 19, 1964), 8.

15. "Borges at N.Y.U.," *TriQuarterly*, 25 (Fall, 1972), 448.

16. "A note on (toward) Bernard Shaw," *Labyrinths*, p. 213.

17. "Borges and the Kabbalah," *TriQuarterly*, 25 (Fall, 1972), 248–255.

18. "The Labyrinth of Time and Place in Two Stories by Jorge Luis Borges," *Hispania*, 45: 4 (December, 1962), 630.

19. "The Labyrinths of Jorge Luis Borges," *Modern Language Quarterly*, 20 (September, 1969), 266.

20. "An Interview with Jorge Luis Borges," *Contemporary Literature*, 11: 3 (Summer, 1970), 317.

21. "Borges at N.Y.U.," *TriQuarterly* 25 (Fall, 1972), 447.

22. Quoted by Paul de Man, "A Modern Master," *New York Review of Books*, 3: 7 (November 19, 1964), 10. The Prologue was written in 1954.

Vladimir Nabokov

1. Minneapolis: University of Minnesota Press, 1971.

2. L. S. Dembo, ed., *Nabokov: The Man and His Work* (Madison: University of Wisconsin Press, 1967), p. 28.

3. "The Flaunting of Artifice in Vladimir Nabokov and Jorge Luis Borges" in *Nabokov: The Man and His Work*, p. 214.

4. *Nabokov: His Life in Art* (Boston: Little, Brown, 1967), p. 300.

5. *Escape into Aesthetics* (New York: Apollo Editions, 1966), p. 129.

6. For Nabokov, too, I will use the common paperback editions for the sake of convenience: The Fawcett Crest *Ada* (p. 425 for this quotation) and *Lolita*, the Lancer *Pale Fire* and the Pyramid *Speak, Memory*.

7. 41 (Summer–Fall, 1967), 96.

8. "The Mechanics of *Pale Fire*," 17 (Winter, 1970), 147.

9. "Vladimir Nabokov's *Pale Fire*," *Encounter*, 19 (October, 1962), 77.

10. (New York: McGraw-Hill, 1970), p. xxii.

11. (Bloomington: University of Indiana Press, 1966), p. 106ff.

12. "Vladimir Nabokov: An Interview," *Paris Review*, 41 (Summer–Fall, 1967), 101.

13. In the order mentioned "Van Loves Ada, Ada Loves Van," *New Yorker*, 45 (August 2, 1969), 67–75; "Nabokov's Ardor," *Commentary*, 48: 2 (August, 1969), 47, 50; "*Ada* Described," *TriQuarterly*, 17 (Winter, 1970), 160–186; "*Ada* as Wonderland," *Russian Literature Triquarterly* (Spring, 1972), 399–430.

14. "Lolita Lepidoptera," *New World Writing*, 16 (1960), 58–84.

15. "Nabokov's Ardor," *Commentary*, 48: 2 (August, 1969), 49.

16. "In the Mind of Nabokov," *Saturday Review*, 52: 19 (May 10, 1969), 29.

17. "Synesthesia, Polychromatism, and Nabokov," *Russian Literature Triquarterly* (Spring, 1972), 378–397.

John Barth

1. Again I will use, when possible, easily obtained paperback editions: Avon's *The Floating Opera*, Bantam's *The End of the Road* and *Lost in the Funhouse*, Grosset and Dunlap's *The Sot-Weed Factor* and Fawcett Crest's *Giles Goat-Boy*. *Chimera* is in a Random House hard cover only.

2. *John Barth* (Minneapolis: University of Minnesota Press, 1970), p. 30.

3. "John Barth: An Interview," *Wisconsin Studies in Contemporary Literature*, 6: 1 (Winter–Spring, 1965), 8.

4. *Kenyon Review*, 22 (Winter, 1960), 104–110.

5. Reprinted from *Book Week* (September 26, 1965), in *The Sense of the Sixties*, ed. Edward Quinn and Paul J. Dolan (New York: Free Press, 1968), p. 440.

6. *The Fabulators* (New York: Oxford University, 1967), p. 160.

7. "Amusement and Revelation," *New Republic*, 159: 21 (November 23, 1968), 30.

8. "John Barth and the Novel of Comic Nihilism," *Wisconsin Studies in Contemporary Literature*, 7: 3 (Autumn, 1969), 256.

9. "*The Sot-Weed Factor*: A Contemporary Mock-Epic," *Critique*, 6: 2 (Winter, 1965–1966), 88–100.

10. "John Barth and the Esthetics of Artifice," *Contemporary Literature*, 12: 1 (Winter, 1971), 71.

11. "*The Floating Opera*," *Critique*, 6: 2 (Fall, 1963), 56.

12. Israel Shenker, "Complicated Simple Things," *New York Times Book Review*, September 24, 1972, 38.

Selected bibliography

Jorge Luis Borges
(1899–   )

Major primary sources

1925 *Inquisitions*
1944 *Ficciones* (1962 Grove paperback translation)
1949 *El Aleph* (1970 Dutton translation)
1952 *Other Inquisitions* (1966 Washington Square paperback translation)
1960 *El Hacedor* (1964 Dutton paperback translation: *Dreamtigers*)
1961 *A Personal Anthology* (Grove paperback translation)
1962 *Labyrinths* (New Directions paperback translation)
1969 *The Book of Imaginary Beings* (Discus paperback translation)
1970 *The Aleph and Other Stories* (Bantam paperback translation)
1971 *Extraordinary Tales* (Herder and Herder hardback translation)
1972 *Dr. Brodie's Report*

"Autobiographical Notes." *New Yorker*, 46: 31 (September 19, 1970), 40–99.

Interviews

Burgin, Richard. *Conversations with Jorge Luis Borges.* New York: Holt, Rinehart and Winston, 1968. Also available as a Discus paperback.
Christ, Ronald. "An Interview." *Paris Review*, 40 (Winter–Spring, 1967), 116–164.
Dembo, L. S. "An Interview with Jorge Luis Borges." *Contemporary Literature*, 11: 3 (Summer, 1970), 315–323.

Dulsey, Bernard. "An Interview with Jorge Luis Borges." *American Book Collector*, 13: 5 (1963), 19–20.
Marx, P. and Simon, J. "An Interview with Jorge Luis Borges." *Commonweal*, 89: 4 (October 25, 1968), 107–110.
Stern, Richard. "Borges on Borges." *American Scholar*, 38: 3 (Summer, 1969), 453–458.

Bibliography

Dunham, Lowell and Ivask, Ivar, eds. *The Cardinal Points of Borges*. Norman: University of Oklahoma Press, 1971.

Secondary sources

Adams, Robert M. "The Intricate Argentine." *Hudson Review*, 19 (Spring, 1966), 139–146.
Alazraki, Jaime. *Jorge Luis Borges*. New York: Columbia University Press, 1971.
Bagby, Albert. "The Concept of Time in Jorge Luis Borges." *Romance Notes*, 6: 2 (Spring, 1965), 99–105.
Barrenechea, Ana. *Borges the Labyrinth Maker*. New York: New York University Press, 1965.
Botsford, Keith. "About Borges and Not About Borges." *Kenyon Review*, 26: 4 (Autumn, 1964), 723–737.
Christ, Ronald. *The Narrow Act*. New York: New York University Press, 1969.
Dauster, Frank. "Notes on Borges' Labyrinths." *Hispanic Review*, 30: 2 (April, 1962), 142–148.
Dunham, Lowell and Ivask, Ivar, eds. *The Cardinal Points of Borges*. Norman: University of Oklahoma Press, 1971.
Enguidanos, Miguel. "Imagination and Escape in the Short Stories of Jorge Luis Borges." *Texas Quarterly*, 4: 4 (Winter, 1961), 118–127.
Foster, David. "Borges and Dis-Reality." *Hispania*, 45: 4 (December, 1962), 625–629.
Gass, William. "Imaginary Borges." *New York Review of Books*, 13: 9 (November 20, 1969), 6, 8, 10.
Hart, Thomas. "The Literary Criticism of Jorge Luis Borges." *Modern Language Notes*, 78: 5 (December, 1965), 489–503.
Lewald, H. E. "The Labyrinth of Time and Place in Two Stories by Jorge Luis Borges." *Hispania*, 45: 4 (December, 1962), 630–636.
McKegney, James. "Buenos Aires in the Poetry of Jorge Luis Borges." *Hispania*, 37: 2 (May, 1954), 162–166.

Montgomery, Thomas. "Don Juan Manuel's Tale of Don Illan and Its
    Revision by Jorge Luis Borges." *Hispania*, 47: 3 (September, 1964),
    464–466.
Murillo, Louis. *Cyclical Night*. Cambridge: Harvard University Press,
    1968.
————. "The Labyrinths of Jorge Luis Borges." *Modern Language
    Quarterly* 20: 3 (September, 1959), 259–266.
Petit du Marat, Ulyses. "Borges as I Know Him." *Americas*, 11: 3
    (March, 1959), 6–11.
Rodman, Selden. "Literary Gold in South America." *Saturday Review*,
    52: 23 (June 7, 1969), 25–26, 36.
Stabb, Martin, *Jorge Luis Borges*, New York: Twayne, 1970.
TriQuarterly, 25 (Fall, 1972).
Updike, John. "The Author as Librarian." *New Yorker*, 41: 37 (October
    30, 1965), 223–246.
Wheelock, Carter. *Mythmaker*. Austin: University of Texas Press, 1969.

Ficciones

Barrett, William. "Mysterious Land to the South." *Atlantic*, 250: 2
    (August, 1962), 141–142.
Bliven, Naomi. "Stunt Man." *New Yorker*, 38: 26 (August 18, 1962),
    95–97.
"Greatest in Spanish." *Time*, 79: 25 (June 22, 1962), 95.
Maloff, Saul. "Eerie Emblems of a Bizarre, Terrifying World." *Saturday
    Review*, 45: 22 (June 2, 1962), 34.

El Aleph

Foster, David. "Borges' *El Aleph*." *Hispania*, 47: 1 (March, 1964),
    56–59.

Dreamtigers

De Man, Paul. "A Modern Master." *New York Review of Books*, 3: 7
    (November 19, 1964), 56–59.

A Personal Anthology

Christ, Ronald. "Borges' *Personal Anthology*." *Commonweal*, 86: 2
    (September 29, 1967), 615–616.
"Journey Without an End." *Time*, 89: 12 (March 24, 1967), 90.
Maloff, Saul. "Moments of Truth." *Newsweek*, 59: 14 (April 3, 1967),
    92–95.
Mead, R. G. "Maze of the Unreal and Real." *Saturday Review*, 50: 19
    (May 13, 1967), 44–45.

The Book of Imaginary Beings

Finn, James. "Relevant Beasts." *New Republic*, 161: 23 (December 6, 1969), 21–22.

Vladimir Nabokov
(1899–   )

Major primary sources

1926 *Mary* (translated 1971)
1928 *King, Queen, Knave* (translated 1968)
1930 *The Defense* (translated 1964)
1930 *The Eye* (translated 1965)
1932 *Laughter in the Dark* (translated 1936)
1936 *Despair* (translated 1937)
1938 *Invitation to a Beheading* (translated 1959)
1938 *The Waltz Invention* (translated 1966)
1941 *The Real Life of Sebastian Knight*
1944 *Nikolai Gogol*
1947 *Nine Stories*
1947 *Bend Sinister*
1955 *Lolita*
1957 *Pnin*
1958 *Nabokov's Dozen*
1959 *Poems*
1962 *Pale Fire*
1964 *Eugene Onegin* (editor and translator)
1966 *Speak, Memory* (earlier version, *Conclusive Evidence*, 1951 and 1960)
1969 *Ada*
1972 *Transparent Things*

Interview

Paris Review, 41 (Summer–Fall, 1967), 92–111.

Bibliography

Dembo, L. S., ed. *Nabokov: The Man and His Work*. Madison: University of Wisconsin Press, 1967. To Dembo's list add the following:

Secondary soures

Appel, Alfred, Jr. "Nabokov: A Portrait." *Atlantic Monthly*, 228: 3 (September, 1971), 77–92.
Field, Andrew. *Nabokov: His Life in Art*. Boston: Little, Brown, 1967.
Gass, William. "Mirror, Mirror." *New York Review of Books*, 10: 2 (June 6, 1968), 3–5.
Gold, Herbert. "Artist in Pursuit of Butterflies." *Saturday Evening Post*, 240: 3 (February 11, 1967), 81–85.
Hicks, Granville. "Man of Many Words." *Saturday Review*, 50: 4 (January 28, 1967), 31–32.
Johnson, D. Barton. "Synesthesia, Polychromatism, and Nabokov." *Russian Literature Triquarterly* (Spring, 1972), 378–397.
Levy, Alan. "Understanding Vladimir Nabokov." *New York Times Magazine*, October 31, 1971.
Moynahan, Julian. *Vladimir Nabokov*. Minneapolis: University of Minnesota Press, 1971.
Parry, Albert. "Introducing Nabokov to America," *Texas Quarterly*, 14 (Spring, 1971), 16–27.
"Prospero's Progress." *Time*, 93: 21 (May 23, 1969), 81–84, 89–90.
Rowe, William. *Nabokov's Deceptive World*. New York: New York University Press, 1971.
Stegner, Page. *Escape Into Aesthetics*. New York: Dial Press, 1966.
TriQuarterly, 17 (Winter, 1970).

Lolita

Appel, Alfred. *The Annotated Lolita*. New York: McGraw-Hill, 1970.
Brown, Clarence. "Little Girl Migrates." *New Republic*, 158: 3 (January 20, 1968), 19–20.
Josipovici, Gabriel. *The World and the Book*. New York: MacMillan, 1971, p. 201–220.
Proffer, Carl. *Keys to Lolita*. Bloomington: University of Indiana Press, 1968.
Rubinstein, E. "Approaching *Lolita*." *Minnesota Review*, 6: 4 (1966), 361–367.
Uphaus, Robert W. "Nabokov's *Künstleroman*: Portrait of the Artist as a Dying Man." *Twentieth Century Literature*, 13: 2 (July, 1967), 104–110.

Pale Fire

Field, Andrew. "*Pale Fire*: The Labyrinth of a Great Novel." *TriQuarterly*, 8 (Winter, 1967), 13–36.

King, Queen, Knave

Appel, Alfred. *"King, Queen, Knave." Commonweal*, 88 (September 6, 1968), 602–604.

Nicol, Charles. *"King, Queen, Knave." Atlantic*, 221: 6 (June, 1968), 107–109, 114.

Ada

Alter, Robert. "Nabokov's Ardor." *Commentary*, 48: 2 (August, 1969), 47–50.

Appel, Alfred. "An Erotic Masterpiece that Explores the Nature of Time." *New York Times Book Review*, May 4, 1969, 1, 34, 36, 37.

Ellmann, Mary. "New Books in Review." *Yale Review*, 59: 1 (October, 1969), 117–119.

Heidenry, John. "Vladimir in Dreamland." *Commonweal*, 90 (May 9, 1969), 231–234.

Hodgart, Matthew. "Happy Families." *New York Review of Books*, 12: 10 (May 22, 1969), 3–4.

Kazin, Alfred. "In the Mind of Nabokov." *Saturday Review*, 52: 19 (May 10, 1969), 27–29, 35.

Nicol, Charles. "Don Juan Out of Hell." *Atlantic*, 223: 6 (June, 1969), 105–106.

Proffer, Carl. *"Ada* as Wonderland." *Russian Literature Triquarterly* (Spring, 1972), 399–430.

Sokolov, R. A. "The Nabokovian Universe." *Newsweek*, 73: 18 (May 5, 1969), 110, 112.

Thompson, John. "Books." *Harpers*, 239: 1432 (September, 1969), 122–127.

Updike, John. "Van Loves Ada, Ada Loves Van." *New Yorker*, 51: 24 (August 2, 1969), 67–75.

John Barth
(1930–   )

Major primary sources

1955 *The Floating Opera*
1958 *The End of the Road*
1960 *The Sot-Weed Factor*

1966 *Giles Goat-Boy*
1968 *Lost in the Funhouse*
1972 *Chimera*

Afterword to the Signet edition of *Roderick Random*.
"Landscape: The Eastern Shore." *Kenyon Review*, 22: 1 (Winter, 1960), 104–110.
"The Literature of Exhaustion." *Atlantic*, 220: 2 (August, 1967), 29–34. Reprinted in *The American Novel Since World War II*, ed. Marcus Klein (Fawcett Crest paperback).
"Muse, Spare Me." Reprinted from *Book Week* (September 26, 1965) in *The Sense of the Sixties*.

Interview

Wisconsin Studies in Contemporary Literature, 6: 1 (Winter–Spring, 1965), 3–14.

Bibliography

Bryer, Jackson. "John Barth Bibliography." *Critique*, 6: 2 (Fall, 1963), 86–89.

Secondary sources

"Existentialist Comedian." *Time*, 89: 11 (March 17, 1967), 109.
Gross, Beverly. "The Anti-Novels of John Barth." *Chicago Review*, 20: 3 (November, 1968), 95–109
Joseph, Gerhard. *John Barth*. Minneapolis: University of Minnesota Press, 1970.
Noland, Richard, "John Barth and the Novel of Comic Nihilism." *Wisconsin Studies in Contemporary Literature*, 7: 3 (Autumn, 1966), 239–257.
Shenker, Israel, "Complicated Simple Things," *New York Times Book Review*, September 24, 1972, 35–38.
Stubbs, John. "John Barth as a Novelist of Ideas." *Critique*, 8: 2 (Winter, 1967), 102–109.
Tanner, Tony. "The Hoax that Joke Bilked." *Partisan Review*, 34: 1 (Winter, 1967), 102–109.

Tatham, Campbell. "John Barth and the Aesthetics of Artifice." *Contemporary Literature*, 12: 1 (Winter, 1971), 60–73.

Trachtenberg, Alan. "Barth and Hawkes" *Critique*, 6: 2 (Fall, 1963), 4–18.

Floating Opera

Hyman, Stanley E. "John Barth's First Novel," *New Leader*, 48: 8 (April 12, 1965), 20–21.

Le Clair, Thomas. "John Barth's *The Floating Opera*: Death and the Craft of Fiction." *Texas Studies*, 14: 4 (Winter, 1973), 711–730.

Mandel, Siegfried. "Gaudy Showboat." *New York Times Book Review*, August 26, 1956, 27.

Schickel, Richard. "*The Floating Opera*." *Critique*, 6: 2 (Fall, 1963), 53–67.

Tanner, Stephen L. "John Barth's Hamlet." *Southwest Review*, 56 (Autumn, 1971), 347–354.

End of the Road

Bluestone, George. "John Wain and John Barth." *Massachusetts Review*, 1: 3 (Spring, 1960), 582–589.

Kerner, David. "Psychodrama in Eden." *Chicago Review*, 13: 1 (Winter–Spring, 1959), 59–67.

Smith, Herbert. "Barth's Endless Road." *Critique*, 6: 2 (Fall, 1963), 68–76.

"A Study in Nihilism." *Time*, 72: 3 (July 21, 1958), 80.

The Sot-Weed Factor

Barker, Shirley. "History Is Still Good Fiction." *Saturday Review*, 43: 48 (November 26, 1960), 21–22.

Bean, J. C. "John Barth and Festive Comedy." *Xavier University Studies*, 10 (Spring, 1971), 3–15.

Dippie, Brian. "His Visage Wild, His Form Exotick." *American Quarterly*, 21: 1 (Spring, 1969), 113–121.

Fuller, Edmund. "The Joke Is On Mankind." *New York Times Book Review*, August 21, 1960, 4.

Hyman, Stanley E. "The American Adam." *New Leader*, 97: 5 (March 2, 1964), 20–21.

"'I' Faith, 'Tis Good." *Newsweek*, 56: 9 (August 29, 1960), 88–89.

Miller, Russell H. *"The Sot-Weed Factor." Critique,* 8: 2 (Winter, 1965–1966), 88–100.

Rovit, Earl. "The Novel as Parody." *Critique,* 6: 2 (Fall, 1963), 77–85.

Southern, Terry. "New Trends and Old Hats." *Nation,* 191 (November 19, 1960), 381.

Sutcliffe, Denham. "Worth a Guilty Conscience." *Kenyon Review,* 23: 1 (Winter, 1961), 181–184.

"The Virgin Laureate." *Time,* 76: 10 (September 5, 1960), 77.

Giles Goat-Boy

Balliett, Whitney. "Rub-a-Dub-Dub." *New Yorker,* 42: 2 (December 10, 1966), 234.

"Black Bible." *Time,* 88: 6 (August 5, 1966), 92.

Donoghue, Denis. "Grand Old Opry." *New York Review of Books,* 7: 3 (August 18, 1966), 25–26.

Garis, Robert. "What Happened to John Barth?" *Commentary,* 42: 4 (October, 1966), 89–95.

"Heroic Comedy," *Newsweek,* 68: 6 (August 8, 1966), 81–82.

Hicks, Granville. "Crowned with the Shame of Men." *Saturday Review,* 49: 32 (August 6, 1966), 21–23.

Kiely, Benedict. "Ripeness Was Not All." *Hollins Critic,* 3: 5 (December, 1966), 1–12.

Klein, Marcus. "Gods and Goats." *Reporter,* 35: 4 (September 22, 1966), 60–62.

Scholes, Robert. *The Fabulators.* New York: Oxford University Press, 1967, pp. 135–173.

————. "George Is My Name." *New York Times Book Review,* August 7, 1966, 1, 22.

Lost in the Funhouse

Axthelm, Pete. "Tiny Odyssey." *Newsweek,* 72: 14 (September 30, 1968), 108.

Davenport, Guy. "Like Nothing Nameable." *New York Times Book Review,* October 20, 1968, 4, 63.

"Fables For People Who Can Hear With Their Eyes." *Time,* 92: 13 (September 27, 1968) 100.

Knapp, Edgar H. "Found In the Barthhouse: Novelist as Savior." *Modern Fiction Studies,* 14: 4 (Winter, 1968–1969), 446–451.

Richardson, Jack. "Amusement and Revelation." *New Republic,* 159: 21 (November 23, 1968), 34–35.

Chimera

Lehman-Haupt, Christopher. "Found In the Funhouse." *New York Times Book Review*, September 20, 1972, 45.

Michaels, Leonard. *"Chimera,"* *New York Times Book Review*, September 24, 1972, 35–37.

Wood, Michael. "New Fall Fiction." *New York Review of Books*, 19: 6 (October 19, 1972), 33–37.

Index